THE UNIVERSITY OF
WINCHEST

BEYOND TRUST

Hype and hope in the British media

D0533253

With Anthony Arblaster, Charlie Beckett, Dorothy
Byrne, Suzanne Franks, Tessa Mayes, John Tulloch,
Nick Pollard,
Ray Fitzwalter – and many more

Edited by John Mair and Richard Lance Keeble

Published 2008 by arima publishing

www.arimapublishing.com

ISBN 978 1 84549 341 7

Printed and bound in the United Kingdom

Typeset in Garamond 11/14

Abramis is an imprint of arima publishing
arima publishing
ASK House, Northgate Avenue
Bury St Edmunds, Suffolk IP32 6BB
t: (+44) 01284 700321

www.arimapublishing.com

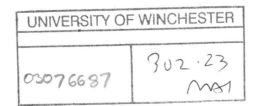

Contents

Editors..v

Foreword: Has trust been restored in British broadcasting?
John Mair, senior lecturer, Coventry University...vii

Section 1. Trust: the idea

1.   The case for scepticism: believe nothing until it
     has been officially denied
     Anthony Arblaster, former Tribune *journalist* 1
2.   Don't trust the debate about trust and the media.
     Question it
     Tessa Mayes, broadcaster, writer..7

Section 2. Trust: can history teach us anything?

3.   Pay-to-play and *You Say, We Pay*: TV trust in a
     historical context
     Matthew Mair, researcher...15
4.   The BBC and trust – lessons from history
     Suzanne Franks, director of research at the Centre for Journalism,
     University of Kent..21
5.   Why did trust fail in the BBC?
     Stephen Whittle, former controller of editorial policy, the BBC.................27
6.   Revealed: Thatcher's role in the collapse of public
     trust in television
     Ray Fitzwalter, former editor of World in Action...............................33

Section 3. Trust today: after the storm

7.   'TV journalism is so fair it makes Andy Pandy look
     dodgy'
     Dorothy Byrne, head of News and Current Affairs, Channel Four.........41
8.   Is the public's faith in broadcasters justified? Yes, it is
     Nick Pollard, former head of Sky News..45

9.   Every PR text book tells you that face to face is best.
     That's the way trust is properly established
     Richard Peel, director of corporate affairs for Camelot...............................51
10. It still has to be proved that declining trust is the major
     factor behind falling newspaper circulations – but we should
     not be complacent!
     Bob Satchwell, executive director, Society of Editors.....................................57
11. Can we trust the internet?
     Charlie Beckett, director of Polis@LSE...63

Section 4. The future

12. Why we need greater transparency about what the media does
     and why and how it works
     Phil Harding, former director of news at BBC World Service..................71
13. 'The BBC has the reputation for being the best
     broadcaster in the world. If they lose that then they're
     screwed'
     Vin Ray, director, BBC College of Journalism...77
14. How changes to HE media programmes can help restore
     trust
     *Roger Laughton, deputy chair of the British Film Institute, former
     dean of Bournemouth Media School*..81
15. Why it's so important to teach 'commitment to
     trustworthy reporting'
     Kevin Marsh, editor of the BBC College of Journalism..............................87

Section 5. Afterword

     Picnics on Vesuvius: the media and the problem of
     trust
     John Tulloch, professor of journalism, Lincoln University..........................95

And finally

     Publication: *Ethical Space* book No. 2 – *Communication
     Ethics Now*..107

Editors

John Mair is an associate senior lecturer in journalism and events co-ordinator for CSAD at Coventry University. A graduate of the LSE, Leeds and Sussex Universities, he is a former producer and director for the BBC, ITV and Channel Four where he specialised in making current affairs documentaries. He is the chair emeritus of the LSE Media Group, director of events for the Media Society and a member of the Executive Committee of the Institute of Communication Ethics. He is the co-author (with Asa Briggs) of *Marx in London* (BBC 1981).

Richard Lance Keeble is professor of journalism at the University of Lincoln. He previously taught in the journalism department at City University, London, for 19 years. His publications include *Secret State, Silent Press: New Militarism, the Gulf and the Modern Image of War* (John Libbey 1997), *The Newspapers Handbook* (London, Routledge 2005 fourth edition) and *Ethics for Journalists* (London, Routledge 2008, second edition). He edited *Print Journalism: A Critical Introduction* (Routledge 2005), co-edited *The Journalistic Imagination: Literary Journalists from Defoe to Capote and Carter* (Routledge 2007) and *Communicating War: Memory, Media and Military* (Arima 2007) He is also the joint editor of *Ethical Space: The International Journal of Communication Ethics* and edited the first volume of the journal which was published in book form as *Communication Ethics Today* (Troubador, 2006) and the second volume as *Communication Ethics Now* (Troubador 2008). He is currently working on a history of war reporting for Open University Press.

Foreword

Has trust been restored in British broadcasting?

Payola in the USA in the 1950s; premium rate phone-in scandals in Britain in the Noughties . Radio and television were rocked to their foundations by both crises. Stations, brands and their on- and off-screen staff trusted by their audiences were revealed to be much less than they appeared. Trusted programmes and names were involved in alleged deception. They had feet of clay. The crucial relationship – that of the audience trusting what was broadcast to their living rooms and treating it as 'the truth' was stretched to the limit

Much of that trust was lost especially once the tabloid press stoked the fire – for blatant commercial reasons – of the 'TV fakery' scandals in 2007-2008. Politicians joined in with their own agendas. It will be a long haul to regain that trust fully.

Did it all matter a fig? Surely the audience expected broadcasters to be 'economical with the actualité' as a matter of course? Did the BBC, Channel Four, Ofcom and, most recently, ITV over-react when programme after programme was revealed to have simply deceived their often high-paying phone in audiences?

Was Auntie too swift to look for penance?
PRC-premium rate phone calls for fair competitions that were anything but was the prime method of deception. There were others. Awards were given despite popular votes, *Blue Peter* cats renamed at the whim of an editor despite an audience vote for another. Was Auntie too swift to look for penance and clean up her act throughout the BBC – she sent all her staff on 'trust'courses? Was the regulator Ofcom using the sledgehammer of large fines to crack the relatively small nuts of a bit of PRC cheating?

The trust issue goes to the heart of broadcasting ethics. If you cannot trust the BBC and *Blue Peter* (of all programmes...) to be honest, then whom can you trust? Worse took place on ITV. The prime time show *Saturday Night Takeaway* (cynics and critics had a field day with that title...) was revealed to have taken money for nothing: £4 million in total. ITV, the broadcaster, was fined £3 million for that. Another ITV show, *Gameshow Marathon*, did the same and was hit with a £1.2 million fine. In total ITV was fined £5.7 million for PRC transgressions. But, should the courts have decided the matters rather than the broadcasting regulator?

This special issue of *Ethical Space* examines the whole issue of trust in the media and the ripples that became a tsunami in British broadcasting in 2007/8. Trust is put firmly under the microscope by a wide range of contributors, many of them distinguished programme makers past and present. They examine the whys and wherefores and try to move the debate BEYOND TRUST.

British TV thinks it has moved on from the self-inflicted trust debâcle. Has it?
Can it?
Should it?

John Mair
senior lecturer
Coventry University
former BBC, ITV and Channel Four producer

- *Beyond Trust: Hype and hope in the British media* is a special supplement to the academic quarterly *Ethical Space: The International Journal of Communication Ethics*. This is published by the Institute of Communication Ethics which has been set up by communication practitioners, academics and journalists to explore creative and imaginative ways of improving standards. For full details on ICE and subscriptions to the journal see www.communicationethics.net.

Section 1. Trust: the idea

Chapter 1

The case for scepticism: believe nothing until it has been officially denied

We cannot trust the corporate media to be objective and unbiased. But, according to Anthony Arblaster, the discriminating consumer can use the diversity of the media and, above all, the range of sources available through the internet, to get beyond conventional and official versions of reality to the often uncomfortable truths they conceal

The great radical American journalist, I.F. Stone, in his later years gave occasional lectures to journalism students. He used to say that he had one simple message that they should always remember: governments lie. That is precise – and true. He did not say the governments always lied. Nor did he suggest that all governments were equally dishonest. Some, and some politicians, are more dishonest than others. But what he did want to suggest was that governments – and not only governments, of course – could not be relied on to be truthful or straightforward. Or, as another famously independent journalist, Claud Cockburn, used to put it: 'Believe nothing until it has been officially denied.'

Sometimes this involves telling outright lies. We have had plenty of experience of this in Britain and United States in recent years, particularly in relation to the invasion and occupation of Iraq. I will give one tiny but typical example. When, after the fall of Saddam, the hunt was on for those imaginary weapons of mass destruction, the British government said that sceptics should not rush to judgement: it would take time to find them in a country 'twice the size of France'. (The reference to France, which was blamed for blocking a UN resolution designed to legitimate the Anglo-American act of aggression, was not accidental.) But Iraq is not twice the size of France. It is not even as big as France. Any encyclopaedia will tell you this. This casual approach to facts, this contempt for truth and accuracy, has been characteristic of the entire catastrophic episode.

Deliberately creating a false impression

Sometimes politicians are more careful. They do not lie explicitly, but deliberately create a false impression. Thus it was never, I think, directly claimed by Bush, Blair or Cheney or their stooges, that the Iraqi regime was responsible for, or involved in, 9/11; but the two were often brought together in a single sentence, so that in the end some 70 per cent of Americans believed that Iraq was responsible for that atrocity. And that was exactly what Bush, Blair, Cheney and co. wanted them to believe.

Often a partial and selective account is given, again with the intention of misleading. This is what the Conservative MP and diarist Alan Clark famously dubbed being 'economical with the truth'. And then there is the matter of timing. The government advisor who notoriously suggested, on 11 September 2001, that it would be a 'good day to bury bad news', was judged to have been excessively cynical, not to say callous, and duly lost her job. But the truth is that she was only pushing common practice beyond the bounds of good taste. Governments habitually release 'bad news' at moments when they think it will attract the least possible attention – at weekends, in the summer doldrums, on Christmas Eve, and so on.

You do not need that much experience as a journalist to be perfectly familiar with all these practices, and with all the myriad ways in which not only governments but all powerful organisations attempt to manipulate the media. They issue press releases, and their hope, maybe expectation, is that journalists will be too busy or too lazy to compose their own copy, and will simply print the text of the original release as if it is their own independent report. In fact, this often happens, and not all reports and not all journalists make it as clear as it ought to be what is the source of the report they are making.

What I.F. Stone was trying to do was to encourage and nourish the two most basic and important journalistic virtues: independence and scepticism. Scepticism can easily shade over into cynicism: a generalised disbelief in every story, an assumption that the truth always lies somewhere in the middle, which can lead to the shallow assumption that atrocities never happen, that outrage is always misplaced, that everything, however inhuman or scandalous, has to be accepted. Such weary indifference is the common trap into which all too many journalists easily fall.

The purpose of scepticism

But the purpose and point of scepticism is to arrive at the truth, not to sit sneering on the sidelines. Inquisitorial interviewers, like Jeremy Paxman and John Humphrys, are sometimes criticised for being overbearing and rude, and it is true that sometimes they bully people who, unused to the public world of the media, do not know how to defend themselves. But overall their performance should be stoutly defended. They play an essential role, they ask the questions of public figures which we, the public, want to ask, but seldom have the opportunity to. They can be far more persistent, probing and effective than MPs usually are when questioning ministers. The rules and rituals of parliament protect governments all too effectively. So the cross-examining journalist plays a vital democratic role. S/he has the role of enforcing answerability and accountability on the part of the government.

The relevant question in this context is whether the media in general are fulfilling their essential role? Are they probing behind the facades of propaganda or spin? Are they exposing the slanted, selective and often distorted and fanciful versions of reality which the powerful constantly try to feed us with? Are they as independent and sceptical as they should be, and as we need them to be?

There is no simple and clear answer to this large question. One of the factors which complicates the picture is the power of the media themselves. I.F. Stone, and contemporary radical journalists such as John Pilger, Seymour Hersh and Robert Fisk, take it as axiomatic that the media should play an investigative, sceptical, oppositional role. But the most powerful figures in the media, above all the owners of TV channels, newspapers and magazines, don't think in those terms at all. Without necessarily having any theoretical or analytical grasp of the nature or power of ideology in society, they understand intuitively that they have the power to shape people's minds and feelings, to mould their view of the world, to determine, extensively if not completely, their knowledge and interpretation of reality. They are relentlessly determined to use this power for their own political purposes, which are nearly always reactionary and obscurantist.

Read the *Daily Mail* or *Sun* for a week: it is impossible not to see that these papers, or rather those who own and control them, have strong, distinctive political agendas. Such an agenda is not primarily promoted through editorial columns, or even by the regular columnists – although allowing for the odd maverick they are clearly expected to do that – but by the choice and presentation of news items. This is clever. We are at liberty to disagree with, or disregard, editorials and opinions. But what is on the news pages is presented to us as fact, not opinion. This is how the world is: asylum seekers (foreign) are being accommodated at airports in five-star hotels, while respectable British citizens (usually white) are being robbed at knife point by violent criminals (often black). The particular stories reported may even be true; what is crucial is the significance that is attached to them. Why were the asylum-seekers so accommodated? Is this a representative occurrence? We are unlikely to be told. Without explicitly saying so, the paper will want us to see this episode as typical: foreigners are being pampered, decent white Britons are the victims of 'immigrant' lawlessness.

All newspapers have their own agendas

All newspapers have an agenda of some kind. The same is true of privately owned and controlled television channels and radio stations - conspicuously so in the United States. Alert readers, viewers or listeners, will quickly pick this up and make allowances for it. But however aware they are, they're still likely to be influenced by it. We are dependent on the media for so much of our information about, and understanding of, the wider world. The internet, however, has vastly and dramatically widened the range of media sources accessible to the enquiring browser. For example, Al-Jazeera provides a salutary alternative to orthodox Western perspectives on the Middle East and the so-called 'global war on terror'.

The Western mainstream media are not monolithic, but on many major issues they embody a consensus which articulates the dominant ideology. Throughout most of the twentieth century anti-Communism was central to that dominant ideology in the Western world and this was faithfully reflected in most of the media. If something or someone could be dubbed 'communist', that was enough to damn them in the eyes of the great majority, just as today the word 'terrorist' is attached to any group or individual whom a government or regime wishes to discredit, and the media in general tend to follow suit.

So far the tendency of this response is clear: we are dependent on the media for vital information about and understanding of the world. It is hard, sometimes impossible, to escape this dependency. Yet most media have their own agenda which determines what they tell us and how they present it. We cannot trust them to be objective and unbiased. We need to be aware of our dependency and the extent to which we are the objects of would-be manipulators.

But, in spite of everything, the media are not monolithic. Two factors militate against this. One is competition, and partly thanks to the internet this competition is now global rather than local. If a good story is circulating, no matter how inconvenient or embarrassing it may be to the powerful, every news channel will want to run it, if only out of fear of being made to look foolish or cowardly by their less deferential rivals.

The other is inherent in the nature of the 'mind industry', as it was called by Hans Magnus Enzensberger. By its nature it cannot be a wholly mechanised and automatic process. Stories have to be written, analysis and interpretation offered. This requires a degree of intelligence. The mind industry requires minds. Needless to say, countless journalists adapt themselves to the needs of their employers and editors, however demeaning these may be. Many secretly or subconsciously despise themselves for doing so.

A minority of independent spirits

But there will always be at least a minority of independent spirits in the media, who persist in thinking for themselves. It is an area of work which will inevitably attract lively and enquiring minds. Often they find it difficult to get a hearing. Sometimes they are systematically excluded from the mainstream media – Noam Chomsky in the United States is a case in point – but some of them will find outlets in more marginal papers and magazines, and may even gain occasional access to radio, television and film. And through the internet they may be able to circumvent the millionaire-dominated media.

We cannot avoid dependence on the media. We need to be alert to our own weakness, and the power of the media owners and moulders who seek to exploit that dependence. But the discriminating reader and viewer can use the diversity of the media and, above all, the range of sources available through the internet, to get beyond conventional and official versions of reality to the often uncomfortable truths they conceal and are often intended to conceal. For this we have to thank the minority of genuinely independent, un-cowed and unassimilated journalists who fulfil their proper role.

- **Anthony Arblaster was a journalist on *Tribune* in the 1960s. He taught politics at Sheffield University and is on the board of *Red Pepper*.**

Chapter 2

Don't trust the debate about trust and the media. Question it

Tessa Mayes argues that the 'trust obsession' is paradoxically promoting mistrust. The solution is to 'investigate everything and make up your own mind'

The general idea of trusting people – including journalists – is not the focus here. At issue is the debate about trust and the media. It is problematic. Trust is becoming a misapplied and overused term in discussions about what is wrong with the media and how it should re-promote itself. Adrian Monck (2008), head of Journalism and Publishing at City University and author, calls this 'the trust obsession'. A recent Deloitte/YouGov poll of 2,046 people confirmed the problem. It revealed that only 36 per cent distrust television (lower than the 48 per cent who claimed to distrust television last year) and only half of those said they reduced their viewing as a result. By contrast, 86 per cent of broadcast executives believe trust in television has decreased 'somewhat' or 'alot'.[i] It seems media chiefs, academics and commentators are talking themselves into a trust panic.

How has this happened? Problems with the media and its relationship to the public and politicians appear to be one of trust and have some relationship to trust issues. When broadcasting scandals result in resignations and Ofcom fines, TV chiefs have talked of the consequences of 'damaged public trust' (Wray and Holmwood 2007) and describe the improvement of services as restoring the 'contract of trust' (Allen 2007). When politicians accuse the media of using an over-stretched, privacy-invading definition of the public interest in political reporting, these complaints seems to stem from a breakdown of traditional, unofficial and trusted agreements about what is fair game to report on. Yet it's not a breakdown of trust that underlies problems with the media and society. Neither is declaring a new era of trust the key solution. Here's why.

Trust as a buzzword in media discussions is a relatively new term. This should make us automatically suspicious. Before the mid-nineties few media commentators talked about issues such as 'declining trust' or how to 'restore trust' in the media. The big debates were about the paparazzi and the right to privacy of public figures. Issues of chequebook journalism, inaccuracy or the rise of consumer-led news were discussed in terms of financial greed, market competitiveness, the effects of new technology, standards, ethics, freedom of speech, human rights and training. But as issues of trust? Rarely.

The mystical golden age of public trust in the media

When journalists say they want people to trust them, this assumes some kind of mystical golden age of public trust in the media. History tells us otherwise. However trust used to mean the public being able to assume the accuracy of media reports and news values based on an idea of the truth and objectivity. However today the media are asking the public to trust their personal motives and moral probity. Crises in the media are followed by calls for resignations, the employment of new faces or new technical approaches to working practices (Macintyre 2007). In other words the new trust obsessions are focusing on journalists' private qualities rather than their actual public works.

Unfortunately, trying to inspire in the public this degraded form of trust can only exacerbate the problem of mistrust. This idea of trust is based on more subjective, almost unquantifiable qualities about an individual rather than aspects of their works which we can assess more objectively using other information sources. Trust has to be earned not just declared as a character trait. In addition it's harder for anyone to build a firm relationship of trust based on the assumed and sometimes changeable motivations of journalists' character compared to the concrete results of their actions. This unstable foundation underlying contemporary ideas of trust always has the potential to ignite further insecurity about relying on the media, not dampen it.

The difference between new and old ideas of trust is reflected in a changing journalistic presentational style that also exacerbates the problem. For instance, news readers used to appear trustworthy by offering up hard news in an authoritative style. Reporters used to be more forensic in their approach to telling us the facts. This reflected the news value of presenting facts and a clear idea of the truth. Now feminisation and emotionalism have coloured the news, reflecting a more ambiguous, subjective approach to the truth. Today news journalists often talk about what they feel about some event more than what they have witnessed. Even the solutions to restoring trust are presented along these lines: if only journalists could emotionally connect with their audience then trust would spring to life and more people would watch the news. But why should the public trust a smirking news presenter who offers up personalised, flirtatious, small talk in between news stories where the facts and an objective approach are reduced? What the public is supposed to rely on becomes confused and slippery.

Why mistrust is not necessarily a bad thing

Mistrust towards journalists is not necessarily a bad thing. It can be an accurate, useful and necessary outlook. Those in the media should work expecting to be distrusted and work harder to earn the public's trust. At the same time journalists have to be untrustworthy at times, being devious to investigate and scrutinise the world. The problem comes when people don't trust why journalists need to act that way. Yet the work sometimes requires journalists to employ all kinds of methods to deliver stories and present them. Sometimes journalists simply make mistakes. To say otherwise is to apply a tyranny of trust on to the whole media which ignores the way journalism works in reality. Journalists shouldn't be expected to be saints even if some do act as if they're saintly.

The public should question what they're told by the media without blind trust. But what's happening now in the trust panic is that there's an assumption from the outset that all journalists are lying, spinning and sensationalising and that the media is a 'feral beast' in Tony Blair's words (2007). This is mistrust gone mad. If we assume everyone is a 'lying bastard', there's no hope for changing the world.

There's no doubt journalists do bad things at times. The media is a powerful force in our culture and its mistakes provoke major public controversies. However, the media is not the only cause of a breakdown in trusted social relationships and the rise of suspicion as a default position. We have to look at factors beyond the media to understand that and along the way, work out what's really behind the panic about trust. Simply focusing on trust and the media can be unhelpful, even a barrier to what's going on and how to solve it.

For instance, what seems to be a problem about trust in the media is really in part the result of a significant cultural shift over the value of truth. Journalists used to be believed – even if the odd one was found to be lying – because they were assumed to be driven by higher principles such as telling us the truth. As long-held political ideologies and cultural norms collapsed, journalists and others have given up on key, guiding values such as the idea that the truth exists. Instead journalists talk about offering analysis, accurate reporting and emotional connections to their audiences. News programmes are seen as brands merely offering their version of the truth. Many others in philosophy, literature and sociology also proclaim the impossibility of finding the truth based on objective reasoning. Everywhere truth is discussed as subjective and impossible to attain. And perversely, accommodating to this relativist approach to the truth is seen as a solution by some to re-inspire trust.

Why truth needs to be intellectually fought for
Yet the truth is out there. It needs to be intellectually fought for to provide a firm foundation for trust. As Simon Blackburn, professor of philosophy at Cambridge University, argues in *Truth – a guide for the perplexed* (2006):

> There are real standards. We must fight soggy nihilism, scepticism and cynicism. We must not believe that anything goes. We must not believe that all opinion is ideology, that reason is only power, that there is no truth to prevail. Without defences against postmodern irony and cynicism, multiculturalism and relativism, we will all go to hell in a handbasket (2006: xiii).

As a result of the cultural shift about truth it's harder for the public to connect with what exactly they should rely on as the truth as a basis to trust the media. It's no wonder that only 16 per cent of British adults trust journalists to tell the truth according to MORI.[ii]

Another factor behind the panic in seeing everything as a trust issue is the media's focus on political hypocrisy (Black 2008). Although this has been heavily debated and criticised, media reports continue to focus on politicians' sex lives or private, financial irregularities. Public institutions are full of people with private vices according to political reporting as if every mistake originates from a conspiracy, every misjudgment is a psychological flaw. The media isn't the only cultural force to project this. But its presentation of the political world in this way helps create and amplify the idea of a permanent whiff of hypocrisy which results in cynicism – the idea that no politician is trustworthy nor ever will be. Caught up in the hypocrisy maelstrom, this backfires on to the media too. Journalists are accused of hypocrisy as if they can never be trusted, ever. In the process the role of the media in society becomes confused. Journalists are treated as if they should be judged according to the same standards as politicians. Yet it is one thing for a democratically-elected public servant to be asked to resign over an action, another for a reporter to lose his or her job because of a journalistic mistake or an act that provokes cultural condemnation (Welsh 2004).

Accusations about the media's wrong-headed values is also a bit rich coming from politicians who have projected an image of back-biting, disloyalty, driven by careerism and publicity-seeking as much as political ideals. Tony Blair made some fair points about the media's complicity in the culture of cynicism in his speech in 2007. Yet it was he who proclaimed that his government would be 'whiter than white' at the start of his term of office.

Powerful climate for cynicism

The media and politicians have combined to create a powerful climate of cynicism. Increasingly in our society nobody trusts anybody (Land 2008). When the media is claiming the moral high ground by promoting the idea that everyone else is a liar and hypocrite it is degrading public life. In this context, any institution – including the media – is part of a spiralling, negative culture in which nothing and nobody is believed. In this situation trying to recreate trust by flagging it up as an abstract ideal won't work. Nobody will believe the media's new mission statement.

Rather, we need to work out what media and cultural values are worth believing in which will make the public more likely to believe in us. Don't trust the debate about trust and the media. Instead investigate everything and make up your own mind.

Notes

[i] Deloitte/You Gov poll quoted in Report: Execs' trust in TV is lower than viewers, *Broadcast* magazine, 22 August 2008

[ii] MORI poll, 2005 quoted in Polls fuel debate about trust in the media, Reuters blog, 27 April 2006. Available online at http://blogs.reuters.com/blog/2006/04/27/polls-fuel-debate-over-trust-in-the-media/

References

Allen, Katie (2007) Grade on restoring public trust in TV, *Guardian*, 8 August 2008. Available online at http://www.guardian.co.uk/media/2007/aug/08/citynews.itv

Black, Tim (2008) Does hypocrisy have a place in politics? *spiked Review of Books*, 15 July 2008. Available online at http://www.spiked-online.com/index.php?/site/reviewofbooks_article/5512/

Blackburn, Simon (2006) *Truth – a guide for the perplexed*, London, Penguin

Blair, Tony (2007) Speech at Reuters, 12 June. Available in full online at http://news.bbc.co.uk/1/hi/uk_politics/6744581.stm

Land, Jon (2008) Young people 'viewed with widespread' distrust – survey, *24dash.com*, 30 June. Available online at http://www.24dash.com/news/Communities/2008-06-30-Young-people-viewed-with-widepsread-distrust-survey

Macintyre, James (2007) Five leads the fight to restore viewers' trust, *Independent on Sunday*, 31 August. Available online at http://www.independent.co.uk/news/media/five-leads-the-fight-to-restore-viewers-trust-463683.html

Monck, Adrian (2008) The trust obsession, Monck's blog, 28 April. Available online at http://adrianmonck.com/2008/04/the-trust-obsession/

Welsh, James (2004) Andrew Gilligan's statement (after resigning from the BBC), digitalspy.co.uk, 30 January. Available online at http://www.digitalspy.co.uk/tv/a13243/andrew-gilligans-statement.html

Wray, Richard and Holmwood, Leigh (2007) BBC scandals stoking crisis of distrust, say Paxman and Marr, *Guardian*, 24 August 2008. Available online at http://www.guardian.co.uk/media/2007/aug/24/bbc.politicsandthemedia

- Tessa Mayes is an award-winning investigative journalist, media commentator and author. Reporting credits include BBC *Panorama*, Channel 4, Five, ITV, *Sky News*, the *Spectator* and *The Sunday Times* (Insight, News). She comments on media issues for spiked-online, CNN, MediaGuardian, *British Journalism Review* and end-of-journalism.org. Tessa is on the editorial board of *Ethical Space* and a visiting fellow at the School of Journalism, University of Lincoln.

Section 2. Trust: can history teach us anything?

Chapter 3

Pay-to-play and *You Say, We Pay*: TV trust in a historical context

Matthew Mair compares the current media scandals with the 'Payola' controversy that threatened to engulf American radio in the 1950s – and discovers some salient features which illuminate the nature and consequences of the contemporary furores

In the recent furore that has erupted in Britain over the collapse in 'trust' in television, specifically in programmes found to have defrauded viewers, such as *Ant and Dec's Saturday Night Takeaway*, *Richard and Judy* and, indeed, *Blue Peter*, little has been said that puts this crisis in a historical or international context.

I shall attempt to go some way towards doing both, by comparing the current situation to the 'Payola' scandal that threatened to engulf American radio in the 1950s. Whilst it was by no means the first example of an abuse of trust by the broadcast media, there are salient features in this earlier case which may illuminate both the nature and consequences of the contemporary situation, namely; an exploitation of a position of trust, the loss of an audience's 'faith' in broadcasters, and the efforts taken for good or ill to restore it.

From Big Beat to taking the heat

On 9 May 1960, disc-jockey and rock and roll pioneer Alan Freed was among the first in the US to be charged in the so-called 'Payola' scandal, having accepted $2,500 from record companies in illegal exchange for airplay. The term, incidentally, puns on a 'Victrola', a popular LP player of the era; hence 'pay to play'. The rise of rock 'n roll, increased teenage spending power and the influence of popular DJs such as Dick Clark and Murray 'The K' Kaufman had made selling 45 rpm singles big business for American record companies. In order to ensure their products' success in this fiercely competitive and as yet unsophisticated market, these companies, especially the smaller ones, would pay DJs to air their records or, more covertly, give them song writing credits. Thus, any sense of impartiality when choosing which records to bless with precious airplay was lost in the conflict of interest. Moreover, though 'sponsorship' of a record was legal, such shady unannounced measures were not.

By 1960, the forces of American conservatism, led by the American Society of Composers, Authors and Publishers, pressured Congress into investigating the popularity of what were until recently known as 'race records'. Contrite record companies soon divulged the nature of the cash gifts made to various DJs, and before long at least twenty-five were implicated. Both Clark and Freed faced a Congressional Committee on the charges. Whilst Clark's penitence avoided damage to his prodigious career, the other was not so lucky. The fine and sentence were light, but Freed, who had rubbed shoulders with Bill Haley in the film *Rock Around The Clock*, and Chuck Berry and Little Richard in *Mr Rock and Roll*, saw his career ruined and died a penniless, broken man five years later (Dannen 2003).

Will you still trust me tomorrow?

What was the essence of the scandal, and where was trust violated by the DJs and record companies? Popular criteria for identifying instances of trust, as used by Bachmann, Zaheer et al., are a belief by the trustor in the honesty, competence and benevolence of the other party (Bachmann and Zaheer 2006). It was the first of these three that was most conspicuously violated by 'Payola'; in concealing from the public the motive for giving airtime to certain songs, the DJs profited through exploiting the trust their audience had in them.

But it would be difficult to say that any listener 'lost out', at least financially, for although the records were popularised, no-one was compelled to buy a product they did not want, but merely had their tastes influenced; Freed maintained under oath, and his biographer concurs, that he had only ever pushed records he truly liked (Jackson 1991). Moreover, the records spun were very popular. It is thus reasonable to conclude that, although their characters were stained, the DJs' basic competence and benevolence in reflecting the tastes of young America must have been less in doubt. Indeed, before the scandal erupted, audiences were arguably better off in some respects; the birth of the 'playlist', the snatching of content control from DJs, at the cost of the taste of mavericks like Freed, robbed American radio of one of its finer eccentricities.

Looking further into what characterises trusting, in both a person and an institution like a broadcaster, Giddens (1991) identifies a relationship which 'presumes a leap of commitment, a quality of "faith" that is irreducible (to rational calculation of risk and benefit)'. It is perhaps this ethereal quality of 'faith' in what is broadcast for public consumption that was most endangered, although due to the lack of empirical survey data, such a conclusion can only be tentative at best. Certainly, the government's response was to re-regulate the radio industry, in an attempt to restore public faith in tarnished institutions. Nonetheless, it is assured that this loss of 'faith', if it has occurred, is not a merely short-term effect. As recently as March 2007, four radio giants in the U.S. were handed down a $12.5 million fine over 'payola' offences by the Federal Communications Commission. The *New York Times* noted that radio broadcasters had 'long been accused' of such corruption, and quoted one world-weary and cynical source as saying it amounted to 'business as usual' (Leeds 2007). Faith, once lost, is seemingly not easily won back. In a nice irony that history seems so fond of producing, one of the writing credits Alan Freed had garnered, and thus profited from when he played it on air, was to the Chuck Berry hit *Maybellene*:

> Oh Maybellene, why can't you be true? You've started back doing the things you used to do.

Whole lotta cheatin' goin' on

Certain examples from the recent furore over 'trust in TV' bear interesting comparisons to the 'Payola' scandal. As great an authority on the subject as Jeremy Paxman noted last year that 'what links all the scandals is trust' (2007: 8). On 26 June 2007, Ofcom, the media regulator, handed down the first of many judgments it was to deliver, in fining Channel 5 £300,000 for systematically deceiving viewers into believing production staff were winning contestants on *Brainteaser*. The regulator 'considered that this was the most serious case it had dealt with, to date, with respect to a public service broadcaster' (Ofcom 2007), but such sentiments soon seemed wistful. Misery was heaped upon misery in July when Icstis, the premium phone-line cousin of Ofcom, fined Channel 4's *Richard and Judy* £150,000 for pre-selecting winners whilst the phone lines for entry remained open, and charging. A disastrous month was ended with the unprecedented spectacle of Ofcom fining the BBC £50,000 for a faked *Blue Peter* phone-in, the first time any such move has been attempted by a media regulator. More travails followed (see Holmwood 2008):

Date	Body	Broadcaster	Offence	Fine
26/07/2007	Ofcom	Channel Five	Faking winners of *Brainteaser*	£300,000
06/07/2007	Icstis	Eckoh (for Channel 4)	Deceiving *You Say, We Pay* callers	£150,000
09/07/2007	Ofcom	BBC	Faked *Blue Peter* phone-in competition	£50,000
09/08/2008	Icstis	iTouch (for Channel 4)	Fraudulent *Deal or No Deal* phone-in	£30,000
24/09/2007	Icstis	GMTV	Fraudulent phone-in	£250,000
26/09/2007	Ofcom	GMTV	Same as above	£2m
20/10/2007	Ofcom	Channel 4	Deceiving *You Say, We Pay* callers	£1.5m

08/05/2008	Ofcom	ITV	'Abuse' of phone-ins on *Ant and Dec...*, among others	£5.675m
30/07/2008	Ofcom	BBC	Unfair conduct in viewer competitions	£400,000

These instances, and more, range from the seemingly benign, misnaming a *Blue Peter* cat 'Socks' rather than 'Cookie', despite the majority of viewers' votes to the contrary, to the frankly astonishing level of cynicism shown by programmes such as *Ant and Dec's Saturday Night Takeaway*, which 'deliberately chose to put entertainment above the trust of the audience' (Ofcom 2008), where winners of competitions were pre-selected by geographical location, 'bubbly' personality or looks, all whilst paying callers tried, and paid, in vain to enter a contest they could not possibly win.

Oh TV, why can't you be true?

The two cases are obviously not carbon copies: far from it. In the 'phone-in' scandals that have seemed to engulf TV there is no analogue to the record companies in the earlier scandal; no evidence has emerged of influence from any third party causing programmes to defraud their viewers. Thus, when such fraud took place, as it was first discovered on Richard and Judy's *You Say, We Pay*, the programme makers stood to profit not from sponsorship or bribery, but instead from the viewers themselves. The programme's makers showed a 'reckless disregard for viewers', according to the premium phone line watchdog Icstis (Gibson 2007a). Thus, one crucial difference between 2007 and 1960 is that the belief in benevolence on the part of the broadcaster, one of the three pillars on which trust rests, has been eroded.

Moreover, the belief in the competence of broadcasters has also been severely called into question. In the *Blue Peter* example, the then-editor Richard Marson is said to have lost his job for overseeing the bungling that resulted in the misnamed moggy (Gibson 2007b). Here it is clearly not a case of profiting from any fraud, but rather giving the viewers' preference an added TV 'sheen'. Nonetheless, such a misinterpretation, whilst not malicious, can only be construed as incompetent, undermining the second aspect of a relationship of trust.

Where both cases emphatically converge, though, is in the loss of belief in the integrity of broadcasters. Radio in America is still dogged with the suspicion of a decades old scandal that continues to resurface in various guises. Likewise, although *You Say, We Pay* et al. have re-emerged in 2008, phone-ins are now preceded by an almost farcical deliberation over the *exact* terms and conditions by suddenly serious on-air hosts. For a nation that never thought 'Auntie' could err, the pocketing of £106,000 of *Children in Need* cash was bitter medicine indeed, the taste of which will not soon be forgotten, even after any subsequent sugar pill (Sabbagh 2008).

Losing the faith?

Similar paths have been followed by the regulators in both instances. In 1960, Freed was a suitable scapegoat to demonstrate a purge of an industry-wide corrupt practice. Likewise, Michael Grade, chairman of ITV, speaks of a 'cultural failing' under his watch, and across the medium (see Ofcom 2008). Thus, similar examples have been made, most dramatic the massive cumulative fine levied on ITV itself, and various heads that have rolled, including Marson's.

In the 1960s, the more fortunate DJs escaped with only a slight blemish on their record, very similar to the current situation. Much as Dick Clark quickly divulged himself of all his interests in the record companies whose songs he was so keen on playing, so Grade admitted that Ant and Dec's executive credits on their programmes had been mere vanity, and the Geordie duo's career has continued on its previous trajectory. In both situations, high-profile declarations of guilt have been preferred, in an attempt to persuade the audience that, as the right hand of the industry has offended, so it has been cut off by the left.

The television industry is also striving to restore faith by announcing new codes of conduct, such as the BBC's November 2007 self-denying ordinance over phone-in competitions (BBC Press Office 2007). This effort at self-regulation bears notable comparison with the introduction to American radio of playlists in the early 1960s, to curb corruption and restore trust and probity. This is not unambiguously positive. In much the same way that playlists robbed American radio of originality (Freed's station was said to have played nothing but Frank Sinatra for three days straight after his indictment), so too tighter rules may stifle the spark of creativity which the audience recognizes in programming it is willing to commit to.

Peter Fincham, ex-controller of BBC1, used the 2008 MacTaggart lecture to argue that the regulatory medicine proposed to revive TV's relationship of trust 'may be as likely to kill it as cure it' (2008). If the audience do not feel they are in a privileged position, a co-conspirator in an exciting and mutually enjoyable experience, they are unlikely to reinvest 'faith' in the medium. As Fincham noted, it is not this year's programmes, but 2009's, commissioned in an atmosphere devoid of trust, that will show whether this has been the correct prescription.

The immediate consequences are becoming obvious. Drawing on a survey conducted by Deloitte, the *Guardian* reported in August 2008 that 36 per cent of British adults interviewed 'disagree or strongly disagree with the statement "I trust the UK's television industry"' (*MediaGuardian* 2008). Moreover, 88 per cent of TV executives interviewed for the same study attributed this collapse of trust to corrupt phone-in scandals. It seems clear that a general belief in TV's dishonesty has become prevalent among around a third of the population. But viewing figures, the proof in the proverbial pudding, are barely dented. 'Payola' didn't exactly kill the radio industry in America, either. But these two pieces of data seem to indicate that, whilst people are still willing to invest their time and money in television viewing, many do so with a certain cynicism, without that ethereal quality of 'faith' that has arguably defined the relationship between broadcasters and public for a generation.

Trust between a broadcaster and his/her audience is a very precious flower. Easily gained, once lost it is almost impossible to completely recovery. British television can learn lessons from the transgressions of US radio in the 1950s.

References

Bachmann and Zaheer (eds) (2006) *Handbook of Trust Research*, Cheltenham, Edward Elgar
BBC Press Office (2007) *New Code of Conduct for Competitions and Voting*, 21 November. Available online at http://www.bbc.co.uk/guidelines/editorialguidelines/advice/interactivity/code/
Dannen, F. (2003) *Hit Men : Power brokers and fast money inside the music business*, London, Helter Skelter
Fincham, P. (2008) *MacTaggart Lecture*, 22 August. Abbreviated in Gibson, O. (2008), Regulation could kill TV's mass appeal, *Guardian*, 23 August
Gibson, O. (2007) Ex-Blue Peter editor sacked, *Guardian*, 20 September
Gibson, O. (2008) Record £150,000 fine in TV quiz scandal, *Guardian*, 7 July
Giddens, A. (1991) *Modernity and Self-Identity: Self and Society in the Late Modern* Age, Cambridge, Polity Press
Holmwood, L. (2008) Timeline: broadcasting deception fines, *Guardian*, 26 June
Jackson, J. A. (1991) *Big Beat Heat: Alan Freed and the Early Years of Rock & Roll*. New York, Schirmer Books
Leeds, J. (2007 Broadcasters Agree to Fine Over Payoffs, *New York Times*, 6 March
MediaGuardian (2008) Loves me Loves Me Not, 22 August 2008
Ofcom (2007) *Adjudication of Ofcom Content Sanctions Committee: Channel 5 Broadcasting Ltd (Channel 5) in respect of its service Channel 5 (Five)* 26 June
Ofcom (2008) *Adjudication of the Ofcom Content Sanctions Committee: LWT (Holdings) Limited, in respect of its service the Regional Channel 3 service transmitted across the ITV Network on ITV1,* 8 May
Paxman, J. (2007) *MacTaggart Lecture*, 24 August. Available online at http://image.guardian.co.uk/sys-files/Media/documents/2007/08/24/MacTaggartLecture.pdf, accessed 28 August 2008
Sabbagh, D. (2008) BBC banked £106,000 of Children in Need phone-in cash, *The Times*, 10 May

- **Matthew Mair is a Politics, Philosophy and Economics student at Trinity College, Oxford University.**

Chapter 4

The BBC and trust – lessons from history

The BBC has constantly faced enormous challenges in maintaining the public's trust – and sometimes it gets things wrong. Here Suzanne Franks assesses the corporation's performances in covering the Second World War and the 'Troubles' in Ireland

Keeping trust with its public has always been a preoccupation of the BBC. Yet the corporation has confronted questions of trust in a variety of forms. The most recent crises and challenges have all concerned the erosion of trust in response to commercial pressures. The scandal about the misleading trails about the Queen and the dodgy competitions were ultimately a result of cutting corners in the face of competitive demands – at the very least they arose out of pressures to maintain audiences in a multi-channel world. Serious mistakes were made and the BBC has worked hard to regain public trust.

In an earlier period the challenges to keeping trust with audiences arose from completely different pressures. During the Second World War there was no competition on the airwaves and commercial issues in broadcasting barely existed. Yet the BBC faced two overwhelming challenges, which potentially undermined the public's trust in its output. The first was the simple matter of keeping the audience listening and the second was question of telling the truth.

There were strong arguments from government that the foremost duty of BBC journalism was to assist the war effort and not to undermine morale. The military has a recurring anxiety about reporting; for operational reasons they prefer to control the news agenda and make sure that nothing gets out. Similarly the propaganda effort (in this case the Ministry of Information) can always defend the need to varnish the truth – especially when, as in the first half of the war, the news was unremittingly bad. Early on in the war the BBC confronted the issue of whether its news programmes should tell the truth – at first there was considerable anxiety – but ultimately news bulletins did report information about heavy losses. The public were in any case so aware of bombs falling, ships being sunk, armies retreating that the BBC, to ensure its credibility, had to make the daring decision by and large to tell the difficult truths.

Asa Briggs, in his comprehensive history of the BBC, discusses the way that the balance between truth and security was struck during the opening period of the war and contrasts the evolution of the BBC's policy on reporting the war with the relentless lies and distortion of German radio broadcasting under Goebbels (which was still reporting alleged German victories well into 1945!). Briggs demonstrates that the BBC's insistence upon truth and consistency produced long term dividends. He describes, for example, the discussions over the use of 'black' broadcasting which was favoured by some officials within the Ministry of Information. This involved 'pretend' radio broadcasting, apparently from behind enemy lines. Yet the BBC held out against such techniques preferring to stick to 'white' broadcasting – in other words telling the truth even when it was not entirely palatable. Briggs praises the BBC's resistance to this pressure, arguing that 'ultimately the "black" broadcasters could set out to demoralize the Germans because they were geared to the war machine: the BBC gained in influence because it was always concerned with something more than demoralization' (Briggs 1995: 15).

Report the truth – no matter how grim

This firm belief that (within limits) the BBC needed to report the truth no matter how grim it was continued into 1942 when bad news for the Allies in Europe and Africa was compounded by a series of quick Japanese victories in the east. One British prisoner commented on hearing these reports (via a secret transmitter) in a POW camp: 'If they can admit a catastrophe so openly, they must be terribly strong.' In other words, he knew that audiences could surely trust what they were hearing was the truth – however grim.

This question of broadcasting into occupied territory focused the argument even more intensely. Here citizens could be shot just for listening to the BBC. Under these circumstances, as senior BBC spokesman were to argue, it was self evidently not worth risking your life to listen to a news programme if it would not at least guarantee you the truth. Lives were also at stake in another sense. In the early period of the war when a more 'optimistic' and less truthful slant was put on the news, the BBC was accused of inciting false hope which led to fatal uprisings amongst resistance groups. The BBC was viewed by the propaganda effort as a means of stimulating potential insurgency – but those who did rise up in the early months and years were doomed because the prospects were so hopeless. It took some time before the BBC realised that its greatest contribution to the war effort both at home and abroad was to provide news that was truthful. A moving testament to this came later from the French socialist leader Leon Blum, who spent much of the war in a concentration camp where he managed (clandestinely) to hear BBC broadcasts. He observed after the war that 'in a world of poison the BBC became the great antiseptic'.

The other crucial question of trust during wartime was in keeping audiences listening. At the start of the war the radio diet placed patriotism ahead of interest. There was a single channel and it was filled with public service announcements, ministerial pep talks (13 already by the fifth week of the war!) and uplifting music on gramophone records interspersed with recordings from a theatre organ. Asa Briggs describes how the public complaints about such tedious output went from rueful to clamorous within weeks. The press too joined in, declaring that 'No emergency could justify such programming poverty' (Briggs 1985: 177). There was such an outcry that by the end of the first month of the war the matter of the dreary scheduling became the topic of a Parliamentary debate. No less a spokesman than Clement Attlee joined in, admitting that 'I am not a habitual listener but I must say that at times I feel depressed when I listen in. You should not be depressed by listening in' (Hansard 1939).

Radical change of policy

The BBC knew that at a time of national emergency it was vital that audiences should keep listening. Yet according to Briggs (1995: 68) the way that the original wartime schedules were devised meant that 'broadcasting seemed inadequate to reflect peoples mood or to change it'. The result of the dissatisfaction was a radical change in policy. Instead of didactic announcements and boring gramophone records, an interesting and eclectic mix of entertainment, information and features was devised from studios based across the nation. Classic variety material such as the legendary *ITMA* (*It's That Man Again*) or the *Kentucky Minstrels* combined with an expanded *Children's Hour* and informative strands such as the *Brains Trust* as well as nostalgic features, were introduced into the schedule. This became the prelude in Briggs view to 'one of the richest and most exciting phases in the history of radio' (ibid: 97) and in particular the variety schedules became a key part of the Light programme, which was eventually the forerunner to Radio 2.

Michael Balfour describes the way that the BBC negotiated this balance between responding to the Ministry of Information and keeping listeners on-side. 'The Press knows that it will go bankrupt unless it gives its readers what they like...The BBC in wartime had a monopoly and secure finances, but that did not remove the desirability of its representing within the bounds set by the national will to win, a plurality of views' (Balfour 1979: 88) – in other words, more varied and interesting programmes. After the fiasco of the early weeks of wartime broadcasting, the BBC realised that it needed above all to keep faith with its audience, which had switched off en masse in response to the unappealing schedule. As a result, programme controllers moved swiftly to rebuild trust from the public and to provide a service that people wanted to listen to again (ibid: 97).

Maintaining regional trust – Ireland

Some decades later, in a very different environment, the BBC again lost trust with an audience and had to work hard to rebuild it. On this occasion it was a distinct group which felt that the BBC had let it down – the Catholic population of Northern Ireland. Indeed the strong bias in representation and reporting by the so-called national broadcaster in the period before the 'Troubles' could be cited as one of the causes of the unrest in the first place. The BBC in Northern Ireland just like many similar public institutions rarely employed Catholics and its news was reported from the viewpoint of the majority Unionist community. Catholics paid their licence fee but were effectively disenfranchised from what they regarded as the *British* Broadcasting Corporation.[i] Such was the BBC's allegiance that it was widely rumoured that when the annual 12 July Orange parade marched past BBC HQ in Belfast, the controller of BBC Northern Ireland came out and took the salute!

Slowly, the BBC's employment policies changed and following scrutiny the way it reported the situation became less biased. It started to reflect a multiplicity of voices instead of just the dominant 'Unionist' view. So the BBC went from a position of representing one community to one where it tried to reflect the whole of society, but then neither side was satisfied! In many ways the BBC was left holding the ring on the (invisible) middle ground. The Catholics had always had lower expectations from the BBC, but many in the Loyalist community were now angered by what was perceived as desertion – for example, when the decision was taken no longer to offer live transmission of the annual Orange parade.

But there was another problem which arose from the question of reflecting reality. In a dangerous and volatile environment there were political demands on the broadcasters from London not to promote violent community reaction. There was pressure to emphasise positive aspects of community relations and the negative, especially the scale of the simmering tension, was underplayed. The result was that a 'consensus emerged which had a false basis' (Cathcart 1984: 263). This again failed to keep faith with the audience that mattered most – those on the ground who knew just how bad things were and there was resentment that the BBC was not reflecting this reality. When the violence eventually erupted, the BBC hierarchy realised that its 'positive' reporting had failed and resolved that it had a duty to tell the truth about the scale of communal hatred. Board of Governors' minutes in the mid-1970s noted there had been a 50-year silence on sectarianism. And in the words of the Northern Ireland programme controller: 'For 50 years the BBC in Northern Ireland has deliberately avoided reporting communal strife – but violence has not been prevented.'[ii]

The crucial role of *Talk Back*

According to Pat Loughrey, the first Catholic to be appointed to a senior BBC position and now Head of the BBC Regions and Nations, the single most important programme that started the move in Northern Ireland was a phone-in called *Talk Back*. It began as a loud, opinionated shouting shop. There was political pressure to close it down as it was thought to incite inter-communal violence, but the BBC held steady. After 'about five years of both communities screeching poisonously at each other, they got it out of their system, realised there was a space in which they could be heard, and then they started to listen to each other'.[iii]

Just as during World War Two, the BBC sought to restore trust with its Irish audiences, by honest reporting, even when it was under pressure to trim. 'The BBC had to learn that it did not exist in order to "build the peace" or "build the community"' (Seaton 2008). Here again it is clear that regaining trust became an institutional learning process. During 1939-45 there were no commercial pressures on the BBC – it had a guaranteed monopoly position – but there were other equally daunting pressures. Those in charge of the war effort on the home front and in the military were worried about giving too much away and wanted to divert the BBC towards the 'propaganda effort'.

In these circumstances it was under political and military pressure not to report the truth. Similarly events in Northern Ireland over many years created a climate of mistrust by different communities. Keeping trust is a perennial issue for an institution that is bound to serve a wide and diverse audience. In changing circumstances, such are the multiple pressures on the BBC that it will necessarily sometimes get things wrong and lose the trust of its public. The interesting and valuable question is how it confronts the process of rebuilding.

Notes

[i] Interestingly the level of licence fee evasion in Northern Ireland was the highest in the UK – perhaps an indication of Catholic disenchantment!

[ii] BBC Written Archive Centre: R78/1407/1 Northern Ireland Civil Disturbances Part 6, 16 January1976 to 9 February 1977 Board of Governors Minutes 5 February 1976

[iii] Interview for the BBC History – Volume 6 *Broadcasting Under Siege 1974-87* (forthcoming)

References

Balfour, Michael (1979) *Propaganda War: 1939-45*, London, Routledge
Briggs, Asa (1985) *The BBC: The First 50 Years*, Oxford, Oxford University Press
Briggs, Asa (1995) *A History of Broadcasting – Volume 3: The War of Words 1939-45*, Oxford, Oxford University Press

Cathcart, Rex (1984) *The Most Contrary Region: The BBC in Northern Ireland 1924-1984*, Belfast, the Blackstaff Press
Hansard (1939) House of Commons debate, 26 September
Seaton, Jean (2008) The BBC and Metabolising Britishness: Critical Patriotism, Wright Tony and Gamble, Anthony (eds) *British Perspectives on the British Question*, Oxford, Wiley/Blackwell

- **Suzanne Franks, a former BBC TV producer, participated in the BBC History project based at the University of Westminster between 2004 and 2008, where she also gained a PhD. She was recently appointed director of research at the Centre for Journalism, University of Kent.**

Chapter 5

Why did trust fail in the BBC?

The BBC's former controller of editorial policy, Stephen Whittle, argues that the origins of the corporation's current 'crisis in trust' and the erosion of the 'broadcasting values system' lie way back in the cultural and political changes of the 1980s

Try substituting the BBC for Great Britain in Dean Acheson's famous remark to West Point cadets in 1962: 'Great Britain has lost an empire and has not yet found a role.' It might be stretching the point, but for me it partly explains why the BBC is where it is, and why it also found, much to its surprise and horror, that trust had failed. But to understand what happened last summer (though I suspect it goes longer and deeper than that), politically you have to go back 20 or more years to the Thatcher approach to broadcasting, and socially and culturally to the consequences of the post-war settlement.

After the rude shock of a rival broadcaster (commercial or independent according to taste) in 1956, commercial local radio in the seventies, the creation of Channel 4 (but even more importantly the arrival of BSkyB in the Eighties), the BBC was no longer the master of all it surveyed. The old imperial certainties were gone. Its place in the sun would have to be worked for rather than relied upon. The BBC learnt a harsh lesson from ITV about tone of voice and the need to compete rather than simply broadcast. Nevertheless, in the Sixties and Seventies, the competition, if fierce, was within a framework that imposed public service obligations on ITV. There were still some shared assumptions about both public space and public value, as well an understanding of the ethics of programme making. People were employed, trained and part of a creative culture that was passionate about what should be done and how it was to be achieved.

I don't believe in a 'golden age'. In truth, some of it was rough and ready. Not every programme that was ever made lived up to high production values or high editorial standards. But, as the broadcasting industry developed and grew, those conversations about what was and was not acceptable became ever more important and, of course, became enshrined in documents such as the IBA code or the *Editorial; Guidelines* of the BBC. Just as important was that the progression from researcher, assistant producer, and so on, as well as the ethics of the cutting room, were taking place within a relatively settled and secure (not to mention cosseted) work environment. It was sometimes cosy and complacent, in which the person down or up the corridor counted for more than who might actually be watching or listening, but it did provide a cadre, a self correcting culture and potentially a career.

Thatcher's impact – and Murdoch's

This is not the place to rehearse the events of the Thatcher years in any detail but the impact of her very clear and definite views on broadcasting resulted in considerable change: 'the price of everything and the value of nothing' summed up what many felt. The immediate consequences were, of course, to shatter the cosy assumptions. It led to the break of ITV as it had been, heralded the arrival of the independent sector, protected by quota, and provided a sustained assault on the notion of public service of any sort. Indeed, there was that lingering question of whether there was such a thing as society.

These were all challenging 'nudges' enough. But they were given added momentum by the arrival of Rupert Murdoch into British broadcasting and the developments that would make possible more choice via cable and satellite, and then eventually the internet and digital technology. Put all of this together and the result was very profound change in economic models, business plans, the structuring of the industry and its workforce and, I would argue, the way in which people both thought about content and how it was to be made. Broadcasting became an industry. Mass production replaced hand crafted.

The BBC does not exist in a vacuum. The changes that hit ITV hard and put the highest bidder before the most compelling content had their eventual impact on the BBC. It, too, had to make room for the independent sector. Politically, it was also aware of the root and branch 'reform' that was being taken to very part of the public sector, including education and the health service. The BBC sought a kind of refuge from the full Thatcherite blast in seeking to emulate the NHS model through 'producer choice', making cuts and more cuts to demonstrate efficiency, and taking a new approach to the way in which it hired staff. More and more people found themselves effectively as freelancers on short-term contracts.

But the law of unintended consequences applies here as elsewhere. In plugging the dyke to protect the field, no one foresaw the fact that a more casual work force had less commitment, was not necessarily properly trained nor had the time to worry overmuch about how things were done as long as the programme was made on budget, on time, and more or less as commissioned. Inevitably, hindsight is a wonderful thing. Steps taken for all the right defensive reasons, in order to demonstrate that the BBC was capable of change, could be efficient, was concerned about allowing talent to thrive without its doors, and was ready to engage with its 'under served audiences' through its *Extending Choice* (of 1992) initiatives and a myriad of pieces of research designed to identify the 100 tribes of Britain to whom the BBC had to bring something special, were what seemed at the time both laudable and, in a certain sense, inevitable. But the indirect cost has only recently been revealed through the tribulation of what happens when trust fails.

Broadcasters' obsession with demographics

The seeds of last year's woes begin, in my view, back then in the Eighties with economic and cultural change (underpinned by political necessity), which starts to erode the broadcasting values system. The second major ingredient is the increasing obsession of all broadcasters with demographics. Advertising funded services need to demonstrate they are hitting their targets. A universally funded service also needs to be able to show it is providing something of value to all those who pay for it.

But it is important not to confuse the two. Reach needs to be kept well apart from share. And in any event, the BBC is not trying to sell something but engage with an audience: 'we use our money to make programmes not our programme to make money'. The danger in all of this is that audiences are not engaged but patronised: 'you are a 24 year CD therefore…' It is all very well to recognise the danger of taking working class money to make middle class programmes, but the response needs to be carefully calibrated. The most successful programmes are those that appeal across ages and social groups and have their own editorial integrity. They are rarely specially designed to hit Generation X.

Put that together with the third element of the mix – new media – and you strengthen the brew. Internet and digital technology has provided an explosion of choice (albeit often recycled material) and has led to both a real sense of consumer empowerment and much tougher competition. The need to be seen or heard raises the decibel level. You shout for attention and everything has to be that little bit more. Notice, too, the blurring of lines between fact and fiction. We now have factual entertainment departments, and a lot of fact-based drama. The two cultures of broadcasting are not the arts and the sciences but the informers and the entertainers. When they blur it can become tragic. Producers who think 'drama' is a licence to ignore or tinker with the evidence (see, for example, *Filth*, a 'play' about Hugh Carlton Greene and Mrs Whitehouse, broadcast on BBC2 in May 2008), or who think the show is the thing so forget being straightforward or honest, just bend the rules to get more or better or more lively contestants.

The explosion of interactions

And, of course, new media also brings with it the interactivity package. There has been an explosion of interactions, emails, competitions, and votes, regardless of any actual editorial value, with 'prizes' that barely deserve the name, or votes that mean or prove nothing. Commercial broadcasters spotted a new revenue stream without thinking through the new relationship that it required, while the BBC saw an opportunity to demonstrate that it was in touch and in tune. Commissioners send out a message that combines spice, surprise and sensation with share. Who should really be surprised that in a more competitive environment, with a more casualised work force both inside and outside the broadcasters, that the temptation and the reality came to be to cut corners and to undermine that most essential of all broadcasting values – trust. As Onora O'Neil (2002) put it: 'Deception is the real enemy of trust.'

It is what Catholics call a sin of omission. Few, I suspect, set out deliberately to deceive rather, as they saw it, to 'improve reality in the interests of entertainment'. But the combination of all of the above, plus the fact that society itself plays a little more fast and loose with the truth and with honesty, resulted in scandals that ranged from *Blue Peter* to *Comic Relief* via Six Music and Radio 4. The BBC found itself caught in a very uncomfortable spotlight. All the guidelines in the world, designed indeed to deal with a more fluid workforce that had not necessarily been raised in the BBC ethics academy (now there's a title for a programme), could not prevent a fundamental values failure in some parts of the corporation.

Lessons have been learnt. The staff have been through their *Safeguarding Trust* course, and rated it highly. The course has been maligned by those who have not taken it. You can judge for yourself, as it is publically available, whether it is an exercise in group-think or an attempt to get people to think about how they make decisions responsibly and ethically. Of course, it should not be necessary, but, as we have seen, for a variety of reasons it was perhaps inevitable. The deeper challenges remain. The leaders of the BBC, directors, commissioners and others, need to think about the systemic challenges that lie around competition, casualisation and distinctiveness. If the empire has gone, at least in the minds of the colonised, the territory continues to be occupied. What is the BBC's role in this new digital world and can it be gained without the BBC losing its soul?

References

BBC *Safeguarding Trust*. Available online at http://www.bbc.co.uk/safeguardingtrust/
BBC Trust (2008) *Editorial Standards*. Available online at
http://www.bbc.co.uk/bbctrust/research/editorial_standards.html
Born, Georgina (2004) *Uncertain Vision: Birt, Dyke and the Reinvention of the BBC*, London, Secker and Warburg
Garfield, Simon (1998) *The Nation's Favourite: The True Adventures of Radio 1*, London, Faber
O'Neill, Onora (2002) *A Question of Trust: The BBC Reith Lectures*, Cambridge, Cambridge University Press
Wyatt, Will (2003) *The Fun Factory: A Life at the BBC*, London, Aurum

- Stephen Whittle is the BBC's former controller of editorial policy, 2001-2006. He has been a programme maker and head of religious programmes at the BBC, as well as director of the Broadcasting Standards Commission. He is a visiting fellow at the Reuters Institute for the Study of Journalism in Oxford and chair of the Broadcasting Training and Skills Regulator.

Chapter 6

Revealed: Thatcher's role in the collapse of public trust in television

Ray Fitzwalter argues that the origins of the recent ITV scandals can be traced back 20 years – when a culture of commerce combined with public service was changed for one of ruthless profiteering

There is a view that in 2007 public trust in television suddenly collapsed. It was formed in the wake of an avalanche of revelations which showed that viewers had been deceived by wide scale programme fixing. There was much validity in this opinion – surveys of public views supported it and Jeremy Paxman, speaking at Edinburgh, would describe it as a 'catastrophic, collective loss of nerve'. Despite swingeing penalties of many millions imposed on broadcasters and efforts by executives to restore trust, the old maxim – a long time to win, a short time to lose – seemed to apply.

But this view, based on the drama and immediacy of a bloodrush of scandal across the major channels, mainly associated with premium line phone in programmes where there were ready opportunities to cheat the viewer, is also superficial and misleading. The rot, particularly in ITV, had started many years before.

Across two decades from the late 1980s, ITV gradually exchanged a culture of commerce combined with public service for one of ruthless profiteering. Good programmes and good profits, in that order, was replaced simply by maximum short term profit, a visionless philosophy doomed to failure. This inevitably changed the climate in which programmes were made and put pressure on standards which first corroded and then fell apart.

The scene had originally been set by the Prime Minister, Margaret Thatcher, who attacked and at times refused to recognise the concept of public service. She regarded broadcasting as simply an economic activity in the market place. When meeting a senior BBC executive she had even demanded: 'You take public money, you spend public money. Where is your profit?' She did not see the BBC for what it was – a public corporation. ITV, a commercial network, perplexed her even more and she was moved to anger on discovering that the market did not allocate the ITV broadcasting licences. Such was her intemperance that some ITV managing directors became convinced that she was trying to drive them out of business.

1990 Act – an 'Act of vengeance'

In the early 1980s ITV certainly had its faults – bad labour relations, monopoly trading and inadequate competition. But by the late 1980s all this had changed. Mrs Thatcher instituted an enquiry into ITV labour relations in the belief that it would produce evidence to justify legislating against ITV. When it proved that her complaints were no longer justified, she refused to comment and legislated anyway. The 1990 Broadcasting Act would be described by one of her advisers as 'an Act of vengeance' while her future Home Secretary, Kenneth Baker, commented: 'The only good thing about this Act is that there will never be another one like it.'

The Act severely weakened the broadcasting regulator; sold off the ITV franchises; made it much harder for ITV to fulfil its public service obligations and heightened pure commercial values. Although widely recognised, even by leading Conservatives, as a disastrous failure, the Act also proved to be a watershed leading to a gradual decline in public trust. Such was her incomprehension that Mrs. Thatcher was surprised that the Act led to an upsurge of violence, sex, greed and crime on the screen in the 1990s – all the things she deplored on television but exactly the things that would put money first in a more commercial climate.

Many other things would change too. At the top the professional broadcasters and showmen, who successfully delivered public service broadcasting combined with commercial programming to compete with the BBC, were pushed out. They were replaced by financiers and businessmen who had no interest in or knowledge of programmes, only in making the maximum money by the shortest possible route and crucially much more likely to chafe against the rules.

Inevitably too, down the chain, a new generation of people would come into broadcasting seeking to make programmes only to make money rather than to acquire money to make programmes. Many programme makers, too, would be compelled to leave the broadcasting corporations where they had practised their art in a secure environment. They would be required to form dozens of independent companies becoming small businessmen in the process. Within a few years many no longer knew what public service broadcasting was. The values of ITV had changed.

The writing was on the wall even before these changes worked through. As early as 1990 in a confidential meeting, George Russell, the chairman of the Independent Broadcasting Commission, challenged Granada Television about potential conflicts of interest – would they, for example, consider selling *Coronation Street* to ITV's rival, BSkyB, given their new investment in the satellite broadcaster. Old style Granada executives were shocked at the suggestion. Yet within three years, in an attempt to get more money, new bosses tried just such a move which threatened havoc within ITV. *Coronation Street* would have been locked off to those who would pay more for the satellite; ITV's schedule would have been left in disarray and the majority of the *Street's* viewers cut off from their favourite programme creating a widespread breach of trust.

Comical start to change in ITV values (involving a Mars Bar)
The change in values of ITV bosses began in an almost comical way when Charles Allen, later to run Granada Television and then ITV, held up a Mars Bar at a Granada weekend away. He wanted to know who in his audience knew how much it cost. No one did. Exactly, he said, and neither did the public so you could put the price up and keep putting it up until there were significant complaints.

It was a defining moment, said another Granada executive. The price would be as high as you could shove it – the aim was not to make a reasonable, or even a good profit, but as much as possible. Gerry Robinson, chief executive of Granada Group and Allen's boss, had even bigger ideas. His view was that the ITV companies, which controlled the market in television advertising (already very expensive) should just put up the price and further exploit their monopoly. In 1990 they had been awarded new long-term licences so he felt Granada could safely ignore the regulator and make much more money. It was soon afterwards that Allen threatened to sell *Coronation Street* to BSkyB unless the ITV network agreed to double the price the price they paid for the popular soap opera.

All this demonstrated a change in financial values and it would not be long before it affected standards and then dented public confidence. A decline in ITV's public service commitments and a new, almost violent, emphasis on commercial values forced a change in the pattern of programming. Down went programmes which did not guarantee safe and regular high ratings and up went those that did, especially those which had extra commercial opportunities. It was a recipe almost certain to diminish public trust and the first big bang came in 1994 when Granada Television was fined £500,000, for eight successive offences associated with product placement in *This Morning*.

It was an unprecedented breach of trust described as 'a relentless breaking of the rules' and incomprehensible in that there had been several offences over several months with written warnings from the regulator in between. These had been ignored. Such warnings came in at board level yet no senior executive took responsibility and the regulator, although furious, did not pursue the question.

Minions were blamed and although the fine was regarded as heavy, the episode was guaranteed to engender public cynicism.

So rapacious would Granada become during the 1990s with its emphasis on money first, that the company even resorted to withholdings its four licence fee payments due to the regulator in the spring of 1998. They were due to pay more than £10 million to the ITC but kept the money back to boost the company's half year figures, making good results look even better than they were. They blamed an administrative error for this breach of four licences. It was the same with tax bills, even the electricity account and all this from what, at the time, was one of the richest media companies in Europe with a burgeoning share price in a buoyant economy.

Connection's 'wholesale breach of trust'
The next big bang affected Granada's closest rival in the bid to control ITV, Carlton Television. They would broadcast a major international documentary entitled *The Connection* which had been fabricated with 16 significant deceptions and would incur a fine of £2 million. ITV had never experienced anything so shocking and it would be described by the regulator as a 'wholesale breach of public trust'. Carlton was forced to return eight awards and refund 14 foreign broadcasters who had bought the programme. The regulator even considered curtailing the licence of the responsible Carlton subsidiary.

Manipulating money and manipulating programmes were not the only factors that weakened trust in ITV. Perhaps the network's greatest strength had been its regional commitments. Most of the ITV companies had nurtured their local roots and built up a strong reservoir of public support. But in the 1990s as commercial pressures to maximise profits coincided with expensive management failure costing hundreds of millions, and then with recession, the regional bases were the first and the last to suffer.

As ITV companies amalgamated and retreated to London so they ceased to serve their regional audiences. Regional programmes were repeatedly cut and the network became more remote. As early as 1994 Michael Grade, then chief executive of Channel Four, had told me: 'I do wish ITV would stop pretending it is still doing public service television.' There followed for ITV a long downhill road until Grade, in 2007, 13 years later, arrived with a mission to turn round ITV only to find more skeletons in the cupboard than he could have imagined.

Perhaps the worst was the wave of programme fixing that broke as he stepped over the threshold pushing public confidence to its nadir. Unsurprisingly most of them were associated with cheating viewers into making expensive and pointless telephone calls in competitions which had closed. But then ITV had discovered that it could make more money from the calls in some programmes, than it could from advertising.

Trust in ITV had in fact declined across many years along with other indicators of its plummeting fortunes. ITV's audiences declined much faster than its rivals in the face of new competition. Revenue did the same. Shareholders would find that they could not trust its management because of appalling losses from foolish investments; politicians would not trust them because they reneged on contracts and even authorised the unprecedented option of foreign management as a potential improvement. The problems had all stemmed from the wrong people running ITV with the wrong philosophy.

Today, as the company continues to bump along the bottom it remains far from clear that it can be turned round. But there is hope. It has some new management that cares more about broadcasting values than its predecessors; it still has a residue of programme makers who, given the right climate, will win back public trust but it is unlikely to be in Michael Grade's business lifetime.

• **Ray Fitzwalter is the author of *The Dream that Died - The Rise and Fall of ITV* (Troubador 2008), hardback £19.99, paperback £14.99. He worked for Granada Television for 23 years and was editor of *World in Action* and head of Current Affairs. He has been awarded two BATFAs, one citing 'an outstanding creative contribution to television' and is a fellow of the Royal Television Society.**

Section 3. Trust today: after the storm

Chapter 7

'TV journalism is so fair it makes Andy Pandy look dodgy'

Dorothy Byrne, head of Channel Four News and Current Affairs, admits to being a 'professional sceptic'. But television is worth trusting, she says: at least a quarter of her working time is spent making sure programmes don't breach the regulations

There is a children's game where you have to stand with your back to your friend and then fall backwards with your eyes shut, trusting that she will catch you. I could never play it. I just couldn't trust anyone that much. Even now that I have grown up, I find trust tricky. For example, when having an operation recently, I had to rise up from the trolley just as the general anaesthetic took hold to warn the surgeon of the dire consequences for his career of any slip of the knife. And one of my favourite pastimes is counting the number of lies in adverts. Of course, I have never married. Trust someone with your life? You must be kidding. Journalism is the perfect career for me. I am a professional sceptic.

And that is why I would urge people to be very sceptical, indeed, when politicians in trouble, companies facing criticism, tabloid journalists and somewhat pompous broadsheet journalists tell you that you cannot trust television journalism. Why are they saying that? What evidence do they adduce to back up their claims? And, let's be frank, if your life was at risk, who would you trust – that lot or Jon Snow? Have you seen those surveys about trust in television? The ones with wildly different results? If you saw statistics for a vaccine that were as erratic as that, you wouldn't use it to inoculate your neighbour's pet rat.

I am not urging anyone to have mindless trust in television journalism. But you should be more worried about what you don't see on TV than about what you do see. Let's take the Olympics as an example of how ludicrous television news coverage can be. Much was made of the fact that Britain won 19 gold medals. But the average TV news viewer must have been amazed we won so few. BECAUSE WE WERE APPARENTLY THE ONLY NATION COMPETING. There was a country called 'China' and a couple of others called 'America' and 'Australia' who tried a bit but they didn't stand a chance. Imagine the surprise of the viewer, when a table appeared at the end of the proceedings which showed that a place called 'France' and other so-called countries with names like 'Germany' and 'Russia' had been there all along.

Sceptical about 'media studies'

I should also make clear that I believe children should study proper subjects at school such as history and geography and am extremely sceptical about children learning 'media studies' when they don't even know where Scotland is. I meet people who study ME. I am fairly interesting, especially to my mother, but wouldn't it be better to know how to find Brazil? Because if you don't find out at school, you may never discover. The early maps created by Europeans fascinate those of us who actually got to read books when we were young. What a limited view of the world those map-makers had! How far we have come since! The whole world in all its splendour is now known. Well, not if you watch a lot of the TV news. Most of the world doesn't even exist. Entire continents suddenly appear and then dissolve, depending on whether they are visited by David Beckham. Some countries only get to exist if they are invaded by the United States of America - which is surely a mixed blessing.

OK I am prejudiced. I am lucky enough to work for a broadcaster which genuinely aims to cover the whole world and devotes up to half its news to far distant lands. We are a protected public service organisation and it is unfair to expect others, in this commercial climate, to major on Mongolia. But, my serious point is that what you need to distrust is the limited and narrow agenda of television. Some reports are so brief and simplistic that I can't believe anyone understands them.

But are TV journalists a bunch of liars who should be distrusted utterly? Absolutely not. On this point, I have no doubt. British television journalism is so fair, honest and duly impartial that it makes Andy Pandy look dodgy. We are not just like that because we are nice people who recycle our plastic cutlery. We are controlled by regulations so precise and detailed that I can honestly say that about a quarter of my working life is now devoted to ensuring we don't breach them. This was certainly not my experience when I entered television. I was a producer/director on *World in Action*, a programme so fine that I admit we have modelled *Dispatches* on some of its journalistic ambitions. But we did not, on *World in Action*, as a matter of course, work to the regulatory standards my programmes have to meet now. I do not mean by that that *World in Action* did not meet such standards. I mean that I now work to required standards of fairness, accuracy and balance that are without parallel in the history of journalism in this country and which go far beyond those required by journalists in other media.

Again, I do not wish to imply other journalists do not meet such standards; only that they are not required to meet such standards. And on top of the standards required of us, we have added yet more rules because, in this day and age, we are conscious that we have a unique privilege in being permitted to broadcast to Britain so our standards of journalism should be as high as we can make them.

Exposing Imams – not a great money making enterprise

But you will sometimes read in newspapers that we make up stories on TV to make money and to get ratings. To be fair, those comments are rarely made by journalists because they realise that if you make the sorts of programmes we make, the income generated by advertising is less than the cost of the programme. That is certainly true of *Channel Four News*, the jewel in our crown, which loses £10 million a year, and true of much of our current affairs journalism too. Last year there was a huge row about a *Dispatches* programme, *Undercover Mosque*, which exposed extremism. Some critics said we had made the programme for 'the ratings'. That, again, is a common accusation made by people who don't like our investigations. Our advertising department chortle in the canteen queue when they see me at the idea that the exposure of Imams who call for the murder of homosexuals is a great money-making enterprise.

When we broadcast that programme which challenged both those with evil views and the politically correct, the West Midlands Police and the Crown Prosecution Service denounced us as liars and said we had, for example, 'taken out of context' those who urged people to kill homosexuals or to beat girls who didn't wear veils. Sorry. In what context was it OK to say that? Some journalists, including, I am sorry to say, some of my colleagues on other TV channels, had a field day and repeated that terrible slur. But other journalists, including some TV journalists, most radio journalists and newspaper journalists on left and right wing papers and on tabloids and broadsheets joined the vast majority of Muslim and non-Muslim people in this country who spotted what was going on here. We TV journalists, flawed as we are, still speak uncomfortable truths. When we get it wrong we should be criticised and admit our errors. But those loud voices who want viewers to distrust all television journalism are the same people throughout history who have not liked to hear uncomfortable truths.

West Midlands Police and the Crown Prosecution Service refused to withdraw that slur; maybe so confident that TV journalists are not well thought of. So Channel Four supported our journalists in suing them. We did it with regret because it cannot be a good use of public service television money to sue other public services. But truth matters. Of course, both the CPS and West Midlands Police paid up without going to court. Our journalists gave their damages – many thousands of pounds – to a charity which protects journalists in danger around the world. Maybe Britain needs to learn to protect and appreciate more its TV journalism in danger here.

- **Dorothy Byrne is head of News and Current Affairs at Channel Four Television. Before that she was commissioning editor for *Dispatches*. She joined Channel Four from ITV where she was a producer/director on *World in Action* and then editor of *The Big Story*.**

Chapter 8

Is the public's faith in broadcasters justified? Yes, it is

Nick Pollard, former head of *Sky News*, argues that while television fails consistently to drive the news agenda it still provides information with 'not too much political slant'

Can we trust TV news? Here's a strange thing: 25 or 30 years ago you never really heard this question. I'm sure it surfaced from time to time during earnest academic discussions at left-wing polys but it certainly wasn't a hot topic when TV journalists adjourned to the bar (which I recall amounted to around at least a third of the entire working day, a shameful shortfall compared to our friends in Fleet Street).

At the BBC and ITN, where I worked during the 1970s, '80s and early '90s, we took it for granted that our news programmes would be appreciated, believed and trusted by the millions who watched them – and, of course, limited choice meant the audiences were far greater then.

Not literally all of them, of course. At ITN we used to take turns as 'duty dog' answering calls from viewers after *News at Ten*. No-one – and I'm sure it's still true today – ever phoned to say: 'Well done, a very fair and balanced programme.' It was always to accuse us of outrageous bias, usually on one or all of 'The Three Is' – Israel, Ireland or Immigration. Overall, though, it seemed to us that the public had a pretty fair level of faith in what we told them. Internally, too, there wasn't much critical examination of the product we offered to the public beyond 'What were the ratings like?' and 'Did we beat the Beeb on that story?'.

There's something of a paradox here. In those days fewer channels and no internet meant our audiences were much higher. Far more people relied on ITN and the BBC for their news yet public trust was, I'm sure, higher. Today, with fragmented audiences and fewer people watching the news, there is far more scrutiny and, I suspect, less confidence in the truth and honesty of the output. And that, of course, is not at all a bad thing. Just as journalists must be sceptical about what they're told by figures of authority, so viewers should be cautious at taking media assertions at face value. There seem to me to be two general tests of trust by the public in the broadcasters:

- Are they pushing a particular agenda, overt or hidden?
- Can we trust them to do the job, i.e. assuming their motives are pure, do they have the resources and the skills for the task?

In my view the first of these is somewhat easier to judge. Over the years, polls by UK regulators and others have suggested that the public retains a strong sense of fairness and lack of bias in the country's broadcasters, not just BBC and ITN but *Channel Four News*, *Five News* and *Sky News* as well. In other words they are inclined to believe in the objectivity of what they are told by these organisations. Or perhaps it's more accurate to say that they believe in the 'honourable intentions' of these news suppliers – in other words they accept that mistakes will inevitably happen but that there is no 'hidden agenda' behind them.

Why broadcasters fare better than newspapers

The surveys suggest that broadcasters fare better than newspapers by this test. Consumers still report strong enthusiasm for their chosen newspaper but they accept that a newspaper is more likely to have a political viewpoint to push alongside (and often within) its news coverage. Is this faith in broadcasters justified? In my view, within this definition, yes it is. In more than 35 years in television and radio newsrooms I can honestly say that the issue of pushing a particular political line, party or personality never really arose.

There are two main reasons for this. First, the substance of regulation on this issue, both for the BBC and the independent sector, has been virtually unchanged for more than fifty years. The BBC's Charter and the law covering other broadcasters make it clear that news must be impartial and free of political bias. It's a pretty easy concept to grasp and it's never really been challenged. Interestingly, back in the fifties and sixties, the first generation of TV newsmen who nearly all came from newspapers, seem to have had no trouble at all adapting to this and understanding the importance of it.

Over the years I've worked with, or watched in action, many of the household names of British television news – political editors, heavyweight presenters, senior reporters and the programme editors and producers who shaped the output. They have all shared, with a remarkable degree of unanimity, a commitment to achieve the sort of balance and fairness that successive governments and regulators have sought to impose on broadcasters through those crucial early years when the limitation on channel capacity made airtime such a precious commodity. Of course it's now widely accepted that there can never be such a thing as absolute objectivity and that while party political balance is fairly easily achieved, all editorial decisions are made by individuals and based on a whole raft of underlying assumptions.

This is not the place to list and analyse all those assumptions but a couple of observations are worth making. The first is that most, though not all, of the underlying assumptions of broadcast news tend to a liberal viewpoint. The former BBC journalist Robin Aitken provided some persuasive evidence for this in his recent book *Can We Trust the BBC?* (2007). His assertion is that the BBC and its output has been broadly pro-Europe, pro-immigration, pro-public spending, anti-America, anti-Israel, anti-business and more sympathetic to criminals than the police. Aitken puts the case rather more subtly but his contention is that this has led the BBC's journalism to incline more to a *Guardian*-ish than a *Daily Mail*-ish take on the world. His point is not that these are unreasonable views to hold but that they are incompatible with the BBC's commitment to impartial reporting on public issues.

Newsrooms remain predominantly white, middle class and increasingly young

The BBC rejects this view but it's fair to say that some quite senior BBC journalists have supported elements of this case from time to time. It's also true that despite the efforts of broadcasting managers over the years most newsrooms remain predominantly white, middle class and, increasingly, young. I suspect that in the past couple of decades the average age of television journalists both on and off screen has fallen from about 40 to 30 as older hands have been weeded out and paid off. That, too, tends to contribute to a particular view of the world, not necessarily an overtly 'biased' one but certainly one with a worryingly limited range of those underlying assumptions.

Sometimes the gaps in the television community's knowledge of society are alarmingly exposed. After the 7 July attacks, for instance, journalists floundered around trying to make sense of what was happening in UK's Muslim communities. Later, as support for the British National Party grew in parts of East London and elsewhere, most newsrooms found themselves frankly uncomfortable in reporting stories of strong resentment against immigration with participants willing to express themselves in blunt, everyday language.

That brings us on to the second of our tests: are broadcasters staffed and resourced well enough to provide the news that the public deserves? On the face of it, the picture looks pretty rosy. While many newspapers have been facing a squeeze on cash and jobs because of falling circulations, the broadcasters seem to have had a less traumatic time of it.

Of course BBC news has had to tighten its belt a bit but still retains the biggest newsgathering operation in the world, with more than 50 bureaux around the globe. *Sky News* and ITN, with smaller staffs, have both had great success in targeting their resources at the biggest stories for maximum impact.

But broadcasters, too, are vulnerable to the modern trend alarmingly described by *Guardian* journalist Nick Davies in his book *Flat Earth News* (2008). This trend can be summed up as: 'More output, less journalism, more "churnalism".' In other words while the workload has soared – bigger newspapers, more rolling news, more electronic outlets – the amount of real, original journalism is falling and being replaced too often by recycled, unchecked handout material originated by the PR industry. And that very PR industry, by contrast, is growing at an alarming rate, much of it, of course, now embedded in the public sector and funded by taxpayers.

A quick count in a typical jobs section of a recent Monday *Media Guardian* revealed advertisements for 103 posts requiring journalism, communication or editorial skills of some kind. Of these, only five were for what might be called 'real' journalistic jobs including three for *Guardian* sub-editors and one for a foreign editor at *Channel Four News*. The other 98 were for PR-based roles, at least two-thirds of them in publicly-funded bodies.

PR – neither devil incarnate nor journalism

You don't have to subscribe to the view of PR as the devil incarnate to see the dangers in this. With the best will in the world the PR industry exists to convey information designed to put the best possible light – spin if you like – on a product, service or company. However you cut it, it's not the same as journalism. At the same time several of the bedrock bases of UK newsgathering are declining – local newspapers, freelance agencies and stringers, the Press Association and ITV regional newsrooms are all contracting. This information gap is being increasingly filled by a growing volume of skilfully targeted PR output that is often scooped up gratefully by harassed journalists and reproduced in many instances unchecked or unchanged.

That's the debit sheet. On the plus side, it's clear to me that over the past fifteen to twenty years television news has become astonishingly adept at the skills of event reporting and picture coverage. Technical advances and the development of on-screen skills by presenters and reporters have brought a fluency and continuity that comes into its own when major stories unfold.

The death of Princess Diana, 9/11, the Soham murders, the Iraq War, the London bombings, the Asian tsunami: all of these have demonstrated the unequalled impact of television to convey the scale and drama of breaking news and world events. Modern TV news graphics also provides an ability – perhaps underrated in comparison with the drama of live pictures – to explain and analyse complex issues in an accessible way. What broadcast news doesn't do, rather surprisingly perhaps, is consistently break original stories and drive the news agenda. That's largely – admittedly with honourable exceptions – left to newspapers.

My feeling is that UK television news, certainly the rolling 24-hour channels, will increasingly concentrate on what it does best, provide continuous, live coverage of a small number of unfolding events, while at the same time offering pictures and information to a wider range of electronic outlets. Can you trust it? By and large yes. Of course there are going to be errors and omissions along the way but if you want strong pictures, instant information, and live coverage and not too much political slant, you can rely on television news.

- **Nick Pollard was head of *Sky News* for ten years until 2006. Before that he was a producer and editor on ITN's *News At Ten*. He started his journalism career as a junior reporter on the *Birkenhead News*. Today he is a consultant and chair of the Royal Television Society Journalism Awards.**

Chapter 9

Every PR text book tells you that face to face is best. That's the way trust is properly established

PR expert Richard Peel argues that improving communication is crucial if trust between journalists and public relations officers is to be improved

'Economical with the truth', 'spin', 'hype', 'Friday afternoons are the best time to bury stories': all of these words and phrases tell us something about the public's perception of public relations. There are some writers – the *Sunday Times*'s A.A Gill, for example – who appear to have a pathological hatred for the profession.

PR Julia Hobsbawm (2007) claims that 'journalism's distrust and hatred of PR has become internalised and institutionalised to such a degree as to be commonplace'. She quotes journalist Brian Appleyard, who is firmly in Gill's camp, saying that hacks still naively pursue something they like to call the truth but their problem is that it no longer exists. 'For truth has been destroyed by public relations executives or "scum" as we like to call them.' Appleyard's strong, emotive language is designed to provoke and, is not, in my view, close to the truth.

What is clear is that there is a sense out there that you can't trust a PR man/woman, that they often peddle untruths and that the local estate agent's description of that house with the perfect kitchen, stunning views across open countryside and ample parking space is possibly closer to the mark than the accuracy of the average news release. As the former landlord of my local pub always says: 'There are always more than two sides to a story and the truth is invariably somewhere in the middle.'

At the root of any relationship...
At the root of any relationship is how much you know about the individual and or the organisation. You need background information and, most important of all, contact, before you can make a judgement about whether or not you can establish trust. What seems to be missing in this age of new technology, 24/7 information overload and some dubious facts on the web – though online can also be used as a great tool for checking facts through reliable sources – is any sense that journalists and public relations people are developing the kind of rapport, understanding and trust that existed when they used to spend time looking each other in the eye. At one time this was often over a pint of beer in a

pub before a bottle or two of wine over a sumptuous lunch which could never come to a conclusion without the PR feeling they had sold a story and the journalist smugly retreating with what they thought was a scoop. But relationships, of course, are more complicated than that. As Julia Hobsbawm puts it (ibid):

> Journalism's job may be to seek out the truth that those in power want to hide but its job is also to sell papers and beat off broadcast or broadband competition. It is under huge competitive pressure to tell the truth selectively. Public relations is tasked with getting an issue on the agenda and trying to shape perspectives favourably in the eyes of whoever is the paymaster so it is also under pressure to tell the truth selectively. Both are under pressure to tell the truth persuasively.

The best relationships are ones where the journalist has sufficient trust in the PR to take significant steers to the extent that they may choose not to run a story on his/her advice. It is a relationship where the PR can confidently provide fulsome background so the journalist gets it right but the source – sometimes – is undetectable. It is where the PR knows that the journalist understands the business in question well enough to write authoritatively, knowledgably and fairly about the issues around it.

Owners' fixation with share price

So why is there a widely held view that this relationship is breaking down? At a Media Standards Trust and Westminster University debate on trust earlier this year (2008) Roy Greenslade, media blogger at the *Guardian* and Professor of Journalism at City University, London, declared: 'We're witnessing an imbalance between the seekers after truth and the gatekeepers to truth.' The gatekeepers had, in the last decade, increased their numbers and resources enormously. While, at the same time, news organisations had 'cut bureaux, cut journalists and grown input'. But PR Phil Hall argued that it was the fault of the 'management consultants that pass for proprietors' not the public relations industry. The owners' fixation with their share price and shareholders had led to the decline of standards in journalism and an 'ever-increasing cynicism from the media'. PRs, he said, were the 'antidote to the journalistic flier'.

I was a journalist before I went into public relations. It was a good move because it meant I could tell, when I made the switch, the questions I was likely to be asked and the angle of the story that was likely to emerge. In fact, I became very frustrated over time because the journalists who were asking the questions had not done their research, perversely often missed the story and sometimes refused to understand the basics before they put a finger to a keyboard. I was often willing them to ask the awkward question so they at least posed a challenge.

That wasn't, of course, true of everyone, I don't want to go down the clichéd route of characterising all journalists as lazy. But trust can only be established if journalists and PRs understand each other and work, to a certain degree, in partnership to achieve their mutual goals. I remember on one occasion at a time when I was heading up the public relations for *BBC News* being called in the early hours of the morning by a journalist I thought I could trust. I gave him significant background information on a contentious story and made it totally clear when I was giving him on the record quotes and when the information was non-attributable, off the record, positively not to be quoted. That afternoon, the story appeared with everything quoted and all attributed to me. Trust evaporated.

If you tell a lie you'll be found out

This happens on both side of the fence. If you tell a lie as a public relations person you will be found out. It is simply not worth it. But the onus is on the journalist to be interrogative, to detect the flaws in the arguments and to demand answers if the facts don't add up. It is also up to the journalist to get their facts right and to interpret stories in a fair fashion. Of course, this is a slightly naive assertion in an environment where the vested interests of the proprietors often take precedence and where even the BBC is moving away from impartial reporting to comment. And then there are regional newspapers who are suffering from a decline in advertising revenues and by stripping their editorial staff to the bone are often so grateful for news releases they will reproduce them in full.

The race to get stories on websites or on air also means there is less time for checking and a greater reliance on gleaning information online which is often unreliable. Coupled with a serious decline in investigative journalism, this means that PRs are often shooting at an open goal delivering their version of events without challenge or questioning and, in some instances, taking that liberty to extremes. If that leads to a breakdown in trust then it is patently unreasonable to blame the messenger.

One frustration for PRs which can often lead to a breakdown in trust is the failure of some newspapers and broadcasters to accept that they have got something wrong. There are notable exceptions, such as the *Guardian*, which prominently makes space to publish corrections. But some newspapers don't seem to believe they owe the public the right to know that they have been blatantly misled. And then there's the old trick of printing corrections in obscurely subbed down form, a week after the story has appeared. This makes putting out a story on a Friday afternoon look positively virtuous.

For the journalist, trusting PRs is also, of course, invariably linked to the organisation they work for. The companies with strong brands, loyal staff, open communications, transparent reporting and a communication team that is swift to respond and eager to co-operate and understand the needs of journalists is much more likely to be trusted. Those that are secretive, have staff who are prone to leak damaging information because they are unhappy or resentful will have a PR department in permanent crisis mode fending off attacks from all quarters and sometimes going to the very edge of accurate explanation.

PR – presenting stories in the most positive light

So, there is right and wrong, on both sides of the fence. Put simply, it is the job of the PR to present stories in the most positive light; to be able to put that information into context and to convince the journalist of the merit of the news angle. It is the journalist's job to ask the right questions, to determine the strength of the story and to rigorously check the facts. This used to happen in two-way conversations in person or on the telephone, *not* via email, where messages can so easily be misinterpreted, and very often as an approach initiated by the PR who wanted to drive the story into a publication or on to the airwaves.

This is not about turning the clock back. The pressures of 24/7 news are considerable. But we won't restore some measure of trust until we re-instigate much better communication. Every text book tells you that face to face is best. That's the way trust is properly established.

So how can we improve this climate of mistrust? One of the Chartered Institute of Public Relation's (CIPR) three key objectives is to 'advocate the highest standards of ethical public relations practice, ensuring that our members are equipped with the necessary skills to achieve them'. The institute has also amended its regulations governing this code, enabling proactive examination into allegations of members' poor practice or misconduct.

Let me conclude with the result of the Media Standards Trust debate about the integrity of PR and journalism. Lord Bell, chairman of Chime Communications and Phil Hall, of Phil Hall Associates – the PR team – defeated the journalists, Roy Greenslade and Nick Davies by 164 votes to 59. In this instance, the view of the audience was that it was for the journalists to take responsibility for their faults and not to blame the PRs. We should have more debates of this ilk. Only through dialogue and understanding of the mutual challenges facing PR and journalism will trust be established.

References

Hobsbawm, Julia (2007) *Where the truth lies: Trust and morality in PR and journalism*, London, Atlantic Books
Media Standards Trust and Westminster University debate (2008). Available online at http.www.mediastandardstrust.org, accessed 20 September 2008

- **Richard Peel is currently director of corporate affairs for Camelot. He started his career on the *Northampton Chronicle and Echo* before moving into public relations. For the past 25 years he has held senior public relations positions with the BBC, Independent Television Commission, England and Wales Cricket Board and the Audit Commission. He also ran a communications consultancy, RPPR, for two years.**

Chapter 10

It still has to be proved that declining trust is the major factor behind falling newspaper circulations – but we should not be complacent!

Regional newspapers are read by more than 80 per cent of the population every week. It would be strange, indeed, for newspapers to maintain such massive popularity if their customers did not trust them, argues Bob Satchwell, director of the Society of Editors

I still wince at the memory of the first verbal kicking I earned from a news editor. 'While a name might be pronounced "Smith", it might be spelt "Smyth" – or the other way around,' he boomed, adding the odd expletive. 'Get them to confirm by spelling it out letter by letter,' he ordered.

If a paper, especially a local paper, spells someone's name incorrectly, they are rightly furious and, as my first news editor explained graphically, if you cannot even get a name right what else did you get wrong? Trust in the paper will be undermined. If that happens why should anyone buy it?

My second big bloomer fortunately came just a day later. 'We have an xyz -street in Preston,' said the news editor, 'but we don't have an xyz-avenue.' 'If the paper can't even get the street names right, what else have we got wrong? Why should readers trust us?' screamed the news editor with more expletives and thick sarcasm – both thoroughly deserved.

That was in the days before graduate training schemes, of course. The first week lessons in the basics of accuracy and its importance in building and maintaining trust were much needed by a raw graduate aiming to seek out world-changing exclusives, but in need of a proper understanding of the special relationship between the 'local rag' and its readers.

The T-word is the most important word in newspapers, and indeed all parts of the media. Without trust, audiences and therefore circulation or ratings drop rapidly, quickly followed by revenue and profits. There is no point in finding stories and writing them because there is no way to tell them.

So while the focus has been on television controversies over phone line rip-offs and changing the name of a children's TV pet dominated the headlines, we should never forget the basics. Newspapers have not been immune from the questioning. Their perceived misdemeanours have tended to concern still more difficult areas such as privacy or the reporting of the astonishing, long-running tragedy surrounding the disappearance of Madeleine McCann.

But it is probably the seemingly small errors that most undermine trust. That is because it is the spelling of names, accuracy of addresses or describing an elderly woman as 'Ms' when she is fiercely proud of her status as 'Mrs' or 'Miss', that people notice most because it directly concerns them. And it is not only local papers that commit these cardinal errors. In the last few months I saw a senior officer described in a national broadsheet as a Navy Colonel, and there was a television caption that read 'Detective Chief Constable'.

Need to be doubly careful in the rush to media convergence

All of this means we have to be doubly careful in the fast-changing rush to media convergence. Trust is the key to building audiences on new platforms as much as it is for the old. New editorial production methods mean that staff may be recruited with different skills and may not have been inculcated with the need for accuracy that I learned in those early hours at the feet of my first news editor.

But convergence is also an opportunity for traditional media in which tough-talking news editors are hopefully still preaching the crucial importance of care and accuracy. News flowing on to new platforms operated by 'old' newspapers or broadcasters should have the imprint in terms of the established quality and credibility of the brands from which it flows.

The pace of change in the media has been electrifying, particularly over the last three years since Les Hinton, then Rupert Murdoch's right hand man in Europe, delivered the Society of Editors' annual lecture. He made it clear that after some years of neglect, the internet was important to newspapers. Murdoch had already started pushing his operation in the US into online publishing and Hinton's speech kick-started the UK press into action.

The rush to convergence has coincided with wobbling revenues as audiences and advertising volumes continue to dissipate, and no one can confidently predict just where it is taking us. For that reason, long before the media itself was suffering the bad news headlines the Society of Editors chose 'trust' as the main theme for its 2007 annual conference in Manchester. It was not a decision based on soothsaying or Mystic Meg predictions. It was simply recognition that to the media more than any other industry, public trust and ethics make up the bedrock on which brand values must be built. Alongside the technology there was recognition that new relationships needed to be struck with audiences.

As the revolution gathered pace along came user-created content and citizen journalists. What would the new platforms and new kinds of journalist mean for the coveted, highly polished brands that have taken so long to create and maintain? Readers might be persuaded to trust newspapers' video and audio content and they might also be satisfied that reports on a newspaper branded website would be of a similar high standard to the printed word, but would they learn to love and trust bloggers and ordinary people like themselves to submit accurate reports and images?

How national newspapers have created cherished brands

Creating powerful, cherished brands is not that easy but national newspapers have done it and local newspapers are often the best known name in the communities they serve. Sadly, when one bit of the media gets a kicking some of the rubbishing rubs off on the rest. It is part of the peculiar ambivalence of the public. For decades they have said with one breath: 'Don't believe what you read in the newspapers' and with the next they argue that black is white – because they read it in the *xyz*, saw it on the telly or heard it on the radio. What that has told us about newspapers for well over a century is that they are an important part of everyday culture and will remain so. It does not mean, however, that they can risk being cavalier with their audiences.

Newspapers, and any other media organisations, have to compete to grab 15 minutes of our time. If they succeed they may have a chance of completing a virtuous circle. It is extremely simple: provide carefully targeted, high quality content that the public comes to trust and audiences will be attracted and maintained. The audience provides a platform for advertising which brings in the revenue for profits and to reinvest in the journalism that creates the content.

The obverse, the vicious circle, is simpler still. Give them rubbish that they do not want or do not trust and soon they will be looking elsewhere. There is no chance of maintaining an audience and therefore still less of selling ads and making money. There is no one-size solution. Readers, listeners, viewers, bloggers and Twitters expect to be told the truth and they must be confident that they can settle those arguments in the pub or over the dinner table, depending on the chosen market.

They also want to be sure that what they will get inside their paper, on their favourite website or niche television channel is precisely what it says on the packet. A posh, up-market, former broadsheet is not better than a red topped tabloid; they operate in different markets. Their readers want the content they trust, not what commentators, still less politicians, think they should want or believe.

The balance of ambivalence

When newspapers get it right the balance of ambivalence sways in their favour. Readers become fiercely loyal to their chosen titles. In the best instances the newspaper moves from being not only handy to being really useful and, if they are precisely on target, they become essential, helping readers to live their lives. The most successful are those that re-invest most in the quality and credibility of their content.

Across the nation there are hundreds of local and regional newspapers that despite challenging sales figures, maintain special relationships with the communities they serve. They are trusted to inform them, fight their battles and provide platforms for their views. They tell their readers where to pick up bargains and provide special discounts and deals for their regulars. Unlike fictional stereotypes, their readers expect a knock on their doors in times of joy or tragedy and welcome their reporters in because they trust them.

Strangely the public is often more forgiving of the media than the media is of itself. Take the news embargo on Prince Harry's deployment to Afghanistan. There was much soul-searching within the media but for once there was near unanimous approval from politicians and most importantly the public. Above all it showed that several thousand editors and senior journalists could be trusted with information that was kept secret from government ministers and senior generals for several months

What PM Tony Blair missed in his 'feral beasts' speech

When retiring Prime Minister Tony Blair claimed that journalists were behaving like feral beasts, undermining the nation's trust in politicians, he mistakenly thought that because opinion polls held some journalists alongside politicians and estate agents in public esteem that he would be loudly applauded. He missed the fact that the polls provide more complex results concerning trust. He also failed to understand the lessons of the Hutton report, that blamed the BBC but let off the government lightly. The public thought it was a whitewash and continued to trust the BBC.

In 2002 Onora O'Neill, of Cambridge University, in discussing the crisis of trust across a range of British institutions, lectured the media in general and the press in particular for being unaccountable. Of course, the media still has lessons to learn but the critics miss the fundamentals. Without trust newspapers would not have any readers and therefore they work hard to win their respect. There are many factors behind falling circulations and viewing figures. It has to be proven that declining trust is the major consideration but we should not be complacent.

Trust is hard to earn and easy to lose but half the population still reads a regional or national newspaper every day, while local and regional newspapers are read by more than 80 per cent of the population every week. That is hardly a dying habit and it would be strange indeed for newspapers to maintain such massive popularity if their customers did not trust them.

- **Bob Satchwell has been executive director of the Society of Editors since its formation in 1999. Before that he was an assistant editor at the *News of the World* before becoming the award-winning editor of the *Cambridge Evening News* for 15 years. He started at the *Lancashire Evening Post* where he progressed from graduate trainee to associate editor, winning the Journalist of the Year Award in the British Press Awards and Witness Box Crime Reporter of the Year Award on the way.**

Chapter 11

Can we trust the internet?

Charlie Beckett, director of the media think-tank, Polis, argues that new Networked Journalist of the internet age must have both trust – and relevance

The internet is now a significant and expanding space for news. It has not yet displaced or revolutionised traditional 'offline' journalism, but it is the most dynamic force in changing the way we make and consume news. Therefore, it is right that we should be properly sceptical about whether we can trust the information, analysis and comment that we get online.

All new technologies evoke irrational fears. These dire warnings and dark forebodings are not usually based on experience but on cultural prejudice and pre-existing anxieties. The internet and the issue of trust is no exception. The reaction to the internet has produced panicked responses, which often conflate concepts and make confused ethical judgements. Internet entrepreneur Andrew Keen (2007) is the most outspoken but typical of those who believe that the internet is innately untrustworthy. He argues that much news produced online by non-traditional journalists is low in quality and unreliable. The 'monkies' of online journalism don't have the skills and standards of mainstream journalists and so we can't trust them.

Journalist Nick Davies (2008) adds the charge that the internet is partly to blame for current cost cutting. In the hands of rapacious capitalist management, the efficiencies of digital production are used to reduce journalistic resources. The result is that we cannot trust what is produced anywhere anymore. Jeremy Paxman's MacTaggart lecture (2007) warned of growing public scepticism fuelled by new technology. As the citizen is allowed to partake of media production, he argued, so they would lose any lingering reverence for the media's skills.

Former Prime Minister Tony Blair told us that he had hoped that New Media would end the bitter dogfight between journalists and politicians. However, the result of the internet, he lamented in his 'feral beast' speech (2007), was yet more conspiracy theories and gossip. Even the great philosopher of the public sphere, Jurgen Habermas (2007), has his doubts. His critique of the internet underpins all those other criticisms regarding trust:

The price we pay for the growth in egalitarianism offered by the internet is the decentralized access to unedited stories. In this medium, contributions by intellectuals lose their power to create a focus.

Journalists – and the priesthood of politicians

For years, the above people have been arguing and working for a trustworthy media. Yet it appears that what they are actually arguing for is a media controlled by an intellectual elite, a priesthood of politicians, experts and journalists. I am not sure that was ever a healthy ambition but it is certainly not a sustainable position anymore. All the criticisms voiced above could, and have been, applied to mass media over the last 100 years. They are very similar to attacks made upon other new technological developments such as the arrival of radio or television when they threatened the status quo.

'Trust' was always a fig leaf for power. Now it is possible to see the real nature of the term. The internet means that the journalists have lost their effective monopoly over news production. The means of production have changed and so too has the power relationship. This means that the trust itself has to be redefined. In the past, we asked the audience for trust (and money). There was an exchange of news in return. Thus, the BBC points to 'trust' ratings as a way of sanctioning its public subsidy. Yet, as Adrian Monck (2008) has pointed out, this was not really the whole point of news. News has always been about entertainment, distraction, partisan persuasion, and relativism as well as 'truth'.

There was no Golden Age when journalists were seen as impartial conveyors of reality. Trust was always conditional. Along with politicians and most authority figures and institutions, journalism is questioned now to a greater degree than ever before. I welcome that. Too often in the past journalism has been partial, inaccurate, and downright false. It has been arrogant and complacent. A questioning approach by journalists is a job requirement, but the distain for their subject and audience that some in the media have shown in the past was a disaster for its long-term credibility. The internet offers a new relationship with journalism that redefines trust into something more meaningful and less hypocritical. I think that his is much more valuable than the dangers it brings with it.

There are risks, of course. The fact is that the internet is a vast space, much bigger than the Old Media area. Inevitably, there will be a lot more rubbish floating around, reflecting people's desire to communicate nonsense and spleen as well as facts and analysis. However, there is more 'good' journalism around than before. This is partly thanks to the lower entry thresholds of internet media. Both mainstream and 'amateur' journalists are creating a greater volume of material. Some of it is only aimed at a few people at the end of the Long Tail.

Specialist bloggers, for example, are able to create small public networks that cover highly refined subject areas at low cost and high quality. While focusing on a niche audience they enjoy almost infinite potential reach thanks to the internet. Opendemocracy.net is a good example. Alternatively, 'good' journalism can also find a global mass audience. The *Guardian* now has more online readers in America, for example, than it does in the UK.

Journalism more accessible – but can we trust it?

Journalism is now more accessible than ever before thanks to the internet. Search facilities mean we can find data, comment and reportage on a scale and with a precision that was unimaginable just a few years ago. But can we trust it?

What is interesting is how systems for establishing trust are being worked out online in new and evolving ways. The internet allows the public to become a part of news production in a way that can build trust. Crowd-sourcing allows the media and the public to access networks of expertise and experience. The public has experts and witnesses who know far more about stories than a small band of professional journalists can ever do. This sharing of information builds trust through a process rather than through pre-ordained 'authority'. It works directly, peer-to-peer, through reference, linking and citation. Wikipedia is the classic example of this collective form of self-correction and validation.

It can also be done through what I call Networked Journalism. This is where amateur and professional journalists work together. The most successful internet news providers are the ones that understand the new nature of trust Online. Some of these will be familiar brands such as the BBC or *The New York Times*. The BBC, for example, has managed to integrate vast amounts of user-generated content (UGC) in to its work without surrendering any authority. They make a virtue of their ability to provide a filter for the vast amounts of data and comment circulating online. Networked Journalism means changing from being branded institutions to branded communities built on a trust relationship.

Then there are the independent new media journalists who also have the trust of their audience. Paul Staines (aka Guido Fawkes at www.order-order.com) is a right-wing blogger who is patently 'biased'. But he can be trusted. He is very clear about his views and corrects mistakes publicly. Staines and his readers are highly self-conscious about Guido's role as a critic of mainstream media and politicians. He plays a Networked Journalism role as an intermediary between professional journalism, the political system and the online public. In his own way, he is as 'trustworthy' as the BBC's Nick Robinson. Previously, we had a monolithic, imposed version of reality modulated between a selection of media companies. Now, we have a network of constantly competing narratives in a virtual market place of ideas.

Aspects of the internet undermine trust. Writers can hide behind anonymity. Falsehoods can reverberate in cyberspace long after corrections have been made at the place of original publication. There is a tendency towards subjectivity and relativism that makes conventional ideas of the truth or objectivity even more unstable. But this is the price of giving the public power and choice. It is a price that any progressive democratic civilisation should see as an investment worth making. The challenge for those in the news media industry is to build new structures of trust with the public for the internet. There is nothing wrong with codes for websites or moderation as long as they are transparent. There are plenty of ways that internet users can protect themselves or their children. But old-fashioned methods of prior regulation are based on censorship. They are simply not practical for the internet. Where they are possible, they kill the very creativity that we benefit from.

Take just one example. The photo-sharing site Flickr (at www.flickr.com) is a fantastic new resource with great journalistic value. It enables the public to report visually upon their lives and the world and creates an awesome repository of photographic material. Thousands of new photos are uploaded every minute. Imagine if you had to pre-check the 'veracity' of every one? It would be impossible and undesirable.

Building trust through process
Instead, internet journalism builds trust through the process. Whether amateur or professional the Networked Journalist must understand that if they want an audience they must have trust. I actually prefer the word 'relevance'. By this I mean it in a very broad sense to describe how 'pertinent, connected, or applicable something is to a given matter'. This does not necessarily mean useful or personal. It can apply to ideas or arguments as much as information. 'Relevant' in this context means that the public is proximate to the information. They trust it because it has been mediated through a network which connects the consumer directly with its production. It may be as simple as the opportunity to email a comment or as complicated as a wiki. It is something more tangible than the old paternalistic idealised sense of trust which was effectively a claim asserted without negotiation.

For internet journalism to be relevant or 'trusted' there are some practical and policy issues. Media organisations need to redevelop their systems and re-skill their staff. They need to become facilitators and connectors as well as editors and producers. They will still need to report, analyse and comment. But they should work openly with the public if they want to build in a network of trust. News media managers need to promote editorial diversity that connects their companies with the vast range of communities and interests that make up our lives and our societies.

Governments need to protect 'net neutrality' and encourage creative commons. They need to build greater media literacy in to all aspects of education. This should include a political and editorial understanding of issues such as 'trust' as well as practical skills to use and produce media for the citizen. And it means better technology such as Text Mining Engines harnessed to intelligent search. Verification and authentication could be built into the very process of engagement through the internet.

But ultimately it will be about competition and power. Journalists were always creators of their own version of 'truth'. It was one forged in the heat of commercial competition and institutional power. 'Trust' as an abstract ideal was never essential to professional news media. Journalism requires attention not faith. This is why internet journalism will be judged on its 'relevance' not an idealised notion of 'truth'. There is nothing innately democratic about the internet. There is no inevitably progressive or humane outcome of its work. I recognise that there are those who make greater claims for online communication. But I put my trust in the more modest hope of Networked Journalism, where the mainstream news media working with the public creates a more open and connected form of reporting our world.

References
Blair, Tony (2007) Speech at Reuters, June. Available online at http://news.bbc.co.uk/1/hi/uk_politics/6744581.stm, accessed 13 August 2008
Davis, Nick (2008) *Flat Earth News*, London, Chatto and Windus
Habermas, Jurgen (2006) *Towards a United States of Europe*. Acceptance speech at Bruno Kreisky Prize, 27 March. Available online at http://www.signandsight.com/features/676.html viewed 30 July 2007
Keen, Andrew (2007) *The Cult Of The Amateur*, New York, Doubleday
Monck, Adrian (2008) *Can You Trust The Media?* London, Icon Books
Paxman, Jeremy (2007) Never mind the scandals. What's it all for? James MacTaggart Memorial lecture, August. Available online at http://www.bbc.co.uk/blogs/newsnight/2007/08/the_james_mactaggart_memorial_lecture.html accessed 13 August 2008

- **Charlie Beckett is the director of Polis, the media think-tank at the London School of Economics and the London College of Communication: www.polismedia.org. He is the author of *SuperMedia: Saving Journalism So It Can Save The World* (Blackwell, 2008) and an award-winning journalist who has worked for the BBC and Channel 4 News and is now a regular writer, commentator and broadcaster on media and politics. He blogs at www.charliebeckett.org.**

Section 4. The future

Chapter 12

Why we need greater transparency about what the media does and why and how it works

Journalists seem to expect the right to question all those in authority but become outraged when their authority is questioned. Correcting mistakes does not diminish credibility, it increases it, argues Phil Harding

Ian Hargreaves, the former editor of the *Independent* and director of news at the BBC, most succinctly summed up the essential qualities of good journalism: 'The first job of journalism is to find out, communicate accurately and be trusted'. At first sight this might seem so blindingly obvious as to be not worth stating. But these days some in journalism and many more in the wider world feel these attributes of good journalism have been, at best, carelessly mislaid, at worst, deliberately and wilfully ignored. They argue that there is now a crisis of trust in the media and it's the media's fault.

In his recent book, *Flat Earth News*, Nick Davies is scathing about the current state of his trade:

> ...until I worked my way into this project [the book], I had no idea just how weakened we had become...I'm not talking about journalists making mistakes. Mistakes can be honest...I'm talking about the fact that almost all journalists across the whole developed world now work within a kind of professional cage which distorts their work and crushes their spirit. I'm talking about the fact that I was forced to admit I work in a corrupted profession.

And this from Onora O'Neil, in her 2002 Reith Lectures on trust, about journalistic standards:

> Outstanding reporting and accurate writing mingle with editing and reporting that smears, sneers and jeers, names, shames and blames. Some reporting 'covers' (or should I say 'uncovers'?) dementing amounts of trivia, some misrepresents, some denigrates, some teeters on the brink of defamation. In this curious world, commitments to trustworthy reporting are erratic: there is no shame in writing on matters beyond a reporter's competence, in coining misleading headlines, in omitting matters of public interest or importance, or in recirculating others' speculations as 'news'.

The internet is full of articles arguing why the media cannot be trusted. The arguments range from the reasonable to the wilder ends of conspiracy theory. Among the broader public trust in journalism also seems to be low. The most recent Ipsos-Mori poll shows that distrust of journalists is widespread. When asked whom they trusted to tell the truth only 19 per cent of those asked said they would trust journalists to do so. (Incidentally, journalists share bottom place with politicians with government ministers only just ahead on 22 per cent.)

A crisis of trust is subversive
A crisis of trust in the media is subversive enough but there is a further even more corrosive thought now in play – that the whole idea of trust in the media doesn't matter anyway. This attack comes on several fronts.

The more traditional argument usually comes from the media itself and goes along the lines of – we just give the punters what they want and journalism is only a bit of fun anyway. For those editors in what might loosely be called the Kelvin MacKenzie school of media management, journalism has always been as much a part of the entertainment business as anything else. Little should be allowed to get in the way of a 'good story' and 'ethics' is a county in the east of England where men wear white socks. Even the former *Guardian* editor Peter Preston (not a natural Kelvin man I would guess) is critical of some of the more, as he sees it, high-minded, recent brow-beatings about trust:

> ...once you decree from on high that every report you print or broadcast must be pure, thorough and blameless, you guarantee that some hapless understandable mistake will bring our hopes to dust – and give your enemies a field day. Media men aren't saints; they need to take risks from time to time, follow hunches and their consciences. Weigh them down with the impossibility of error and they turn dull, dithering – and excruciatingly pompous.

New into this field of trust irrelevance are the internet evangelists. Their argument is different. Broadly put it goes – we never really believed in what we read and saw before anyway but with the internet none of that matters because this new digital age is much more raw and authentic so now we can decide for ourselves. This argument has been put by Jeff Jarvis, journalism professor at the City University of New York and internet guru:

> Bloggers are more trusted, I think, because they are human and too often news organisations are not. Bloggers tell you who they are (usually) and what their backgrounds and biases are and their readers can judge them and engage with them on a personal level. News organisations are big and

often monolithic and are reluctant to admit, let alone share perspective or agendas. And the reporters and editors in them sometimes hide inside the cathedral of journalism.

The purposes of journalism

The purposes of journalism are of course multiple: for some it's to make money, for others it's about power, at times it's about being entertaining and diverting. But at its core journalism is about imparting facts, telling readers and viewers and listeners about events that really occurred. Because of this, journalism also has a wider social and political purpose. It performs an important function in liberal democracies. It was Thomas Jefferson who said: 'If a nation expects to be ignorant and free... it expects what never was and never will be.'

Here in the UK, though, we have nothing to match the First Amendment to the U.S. constitution, the special place of journalism has long been recognised. The press are allowed privileged access to parliament and to the courts, though the press benches these days are often regrettably empty; Ministers will regularly come on the *Today* programme to be roughed up by John Humphrys; journalists are given latitude by the courts when it comes to revealing sources for their story. So throughout British public life there is an acceptance that journalists and journalism have a unique place.

The reason that journalists have this access and privilege is based on 'the public's right to know'. This is the doctrine of democratic accountability which says that in an open, vibrant democracy, the public have a right to know what is being done in their name. Press and broadcasting is therefore recognised as an important conduit to the public and hence the electorate. As the veteran American journalist Bill Moyers puts it: 'Democracy without honest information creates the illusion of popular consent while enhancing the power of the state and the privileged interests protected by it.'

The public's right to know also means that the media can be a legitimate check on the abuse of power. Proper investigative journalism can and should uncover scandals and corruption which otherwise might go unchecked. But there is an important qualification in that Bill Moyer's quote and it is his use of the word 'honest'. The relationship between a free media and an informed democracy crucially depends on 'honest information'; without it the relationship breaks down. But what do we mean by honest information?

Towards a new understanding of trust

I earlier instanced several supporters of the idea that trust in the media had broken down. But how real is that impression of a crisis? On the evidence of the Ipsos-Mori poll it is very real indeed. More than four fifths of the population say they do not trust journalists. But look more closely at the poll figures and a more complex picture emerges. While journalists in general are mistrusted, television newsreaders are judged much more trustworthy. 61 per cent say they trust them. In reality there is a more sophisticated understanding by the public of different levels of trust. It may well be that figures are not all that they seem.

And then there is question of what exactly do we mean by trust. In a recent article, Peter Preston argued that it was highly dangerous for institutions like the BBC to set so much store by the word trust:

> Ask yourself how journalism has been (and still can be) best described? Yes as first rough draft of history. And what pray does that mean – if not that countless facts and judgments that come our way every week are desperately frail ….Anything that can be got wrong will emerge tattered and torn…..Trust is as good as the last sentence you wrote. And true trust is making sure the reader knows that.

The shrewd Preston is on to something important here. When we talk about trust in the media we are not describing a state of pure perfection. What we are really attempting to do is to portray a world in which fallible journalists do their level best to give as accurate a picture as they can and understand that their readers and viewers will accept this, provided that they believe an honest attempt (that word honest again) has been made.

Trust does matter

So trust in journalism does matter. It matters because it underpins some of the features necessary for the working of a healthy democracy: an informed electorate with access to honest information and able to check abuses of power and corruption. Without trust in the media then the public will not believe what they see and read and the rest will not follow. So if trust is that important how can we ensure that it can be maintained and built on in the future?

First, it is important that we are clear what we mean by trust in the media; that we don't overstate the ability of journalists to get things right and that we openly acknowledge what an imperfect picture journalism can paint. So a little more humility on the part of journalists and publications will be needed – something some don't take to too readily.

Allied to this, there needs to be greater transparency about what the media does and why and how it works. We also need more openness about regulation. Not more regulation, there's more than enough of that about already. But why not, for example, make the complaints processes of Ofcom, the BBC and the Press Complaints Commission open to the public? Why not hold their meetings in public? It might take some legal finessing but in the end since these bodies exist to serve and protect the public, why not open them up?

Correcting mistakes willingly and generously is also vital. The public will, for the most part, excuse mistakes genuinely made, if they are speedily corrected. This is something most journalists are still notoriously reluctant to do. Journalists seem to expect the right to question all those in authority but become outraged when it is their authority that is questioned. Correcting mistakes does not diminish credibility, it increases it.

Trust in the media by the public is vital. It should not be a blind trust but a conditional one; one in which both sides go in with their eyes wide open. But if journalists disregard this fragile compact then they risk surrendering all rights to a special place in society. If that were to happen then not only would journalism suffer but democracy and society would too.

- **Phil Harding is journalist and a media consultant. He has held a number of senior editorial jobs at the BBC including controller editorial policy, editor of *Today* and director of news at the World Service.**

Chapter 13

'The BBC has the reputation for being the best broadcaster in the world. If they lose that then they're screwed'

Vin Ray, director of the BBC College of Journalism, argues that the corporation must maintain a culture and value system that puts trust and integrity at its heart.

Shortly after six o'clock on a warm September evening in 2007, a small group of BBC executives, myself included, descended into the muggy basement of a Georgian townhouse, just off Baker Street. We were there to witness the first of a series of UK-wide focus groups. The subject: trust in broadcasting. Those of us from the BBC sat, like urban anthropologists, invisible behind a glass screen as the participants were trooped into the room. The session followed a familiar pattern, the moderator skilfully warming up her charges before the real excavation began.

I had commissioned the sessions as part of the response to the problems that had beset the industry over the summer. We were to show them a range of clips from various programmes, discuss how those clips were made and then ask the group, as representatives of the BBC audience, whether they felt that the artifice used in their production was acceptable or amounted to deceit. As well as using the research in its own right, we were filming the groups and hoped to get some useful clips to illustrate the workshops the College of Journalism was designing around the line between legitimate artifice and deliberate deceit. It was clear very quickly that we would get some forceful contributions.

Focus groups get a bad press but they are often salutary and this one was no exception. In all honesty, we hadn't known what to expect. Would they be aware of the scandals? Were they surprised by them? More importantly, did they care?

The group were warmed up with questions about viewing habits, but quickly found themselves ranking broadcasters in to a league table of trust. It is not stretching the truth to say that, across the groups, the BBC comfortably topped the table. What was more interesting was that the *expectations* of the BBC were so much higher than of other broadcasters. The BBC, they said, is different. It therefore followed – and we witnessed it first-hand – that the disappointment in the BBC was all the higher and more aggressive when it was deemed to have fallen short.

Pervading sense of all broadcasters 'on the fiddle'

So what had left them in such high dudgeon? First of all, a pervading sense of all broadcasters 'on the fiddle'. As one respondent put it: 'They're all at it.' But if one programme encapsulated the sense of betrayal they felt it was *Blue Peter*. 'It was despicable,' said one woman. 'A *Blue Peter* badge means everything,' said another, with misty-eyed disappointment. This was the BBC, whom they trusted more than other broadcasters; what's more it was a children's programme; and most of all it was one of the longest established and most trusted brands. And, as we discovered, brands count for a lot. Well-known programmes and well-known presenters engender a greater sense of betrayal when they transgress.

And the spore of mistrust spreads quickly. The misdemeanours had developed a life of their own and expanded like a Chinese whisper. Many thought the documentary about the Queen had already been broadcast (a misleading edit of a trailer had been shown to the press); half the audience thought the BBC had made money out of the phone scandals (though the problems uncovered at the BBC involved no commercial gain). That they cared as much as they did is, ultimately, hugely heartening. As they swung from disappointment through cynicism to occasional anger it wasn't always easy listening. But we were left in no doubt: trust matters.

The discussion moved away from general areas to the specific clips, which had been chosen because they were deemed to be in that grey area where the line between right and wrong is not so easy to discern. The groups viewed each different clip with great common sense. The majority were deemed to be fine, a few unacceptable and a remainder that would have been acceptable had the artifice been flagged to the audience. Typical of this was a clip from *Blue Planet* that had filmed the birth of lobsters in an aquarium rather than, as had been assumed, in the sea. The viewers were initially annoyed, but when it was explained to them that there was no other way of filming this happening, they became more supportive and generally felt that it would have been fine, had the programme found a way of properly alerting the audience to it. The issue in so many cases was how we label the artifice we have used.

Now it's important not to exaggerate or suggest the existence of any endemic malfeasance inside the BBC; the incidents that came to light represent a tiny fraction of the BBC's output. But neither should I underestimate the sense of betrayal these groups felt about some of the programmes.

Trust – the life blood of the BBC

The BBC's director-general, Mark Thompson, said in the aftermath of last summer's events that, 'Public trust is the life-blood of the BBC. Without it, it has no value as an institution.' That, in essence, is why the BBC acted so quickly, decisively – and publicly. A comprehensive trawl through the BBC's entire output was painful and time-consuming and led to staff being disciplined. Some 19,000 staff attended – and enjoyed – the *Safeguarding Trust* workshops, the largest single training programme ever undertaken in the British media. And strict new codes were put in place around the conduct of competitions.

It was tempting to think that this was an over-reaction to some localised problems in a small number of programmes – a bout of unnecessary self-flagellation. But deceit is corrosive. And it has a contagious effect: a breach of trust in one programme reflects on the whole organisation. Early on in that first focus group, one participant said: 'You think to yourself, if they're rigging children's programmes, what else are they manipulating?'

Which brings us to news. Trust is nowhere more important than in journalism and, perhaps inevitably, audiences tend to view the issue of trust through the prism of news more than any other genre. Polls consistently show that, while the public trust broadsheet newspapers more than tabloids, they trust broadcasters more than any other medium. One of the distinguishing attributes of British broadcasting is its obligation to the concept of impartiality. By and large, it is clear that audiences still place huge value on the ability to get their information free from bias and editorialising and with sufficient context and diversity of opinion to make up their own minds.

Polls show that the BBC is the most trusted news provider in the UK by some distance and number one globally, too. That hasn't happened by accident and the Beeb's global reputation for accuracy and impartiality is the defining factor. But if we dig just below the surface of these polls something interesting, and perhaps profound, is happening. The third most trusted news provider, globally? Google. And how much original news content does Google generate? Correct: none.

On a bullet train to a future we don't fully understand

These are challenging times. We are on a bullet train to a future we don't fully understand. The journey to a digital, multi-platform future is transforming the ecology of broadcasting. Old silos are collapsing; producers used to ploughing a single furrow are working across several platforms at once; production teams are getting smaller; a 24-hour culture means shorter deadlines; and the battle to be heard in an ever-expanding galaxy of output gets ever more challenging. The temptation to cut corners or enhance what you've got is greater than ever.

Given these changes, it has never been more important that BBC content producers understand that trust and integrity must always remain the *sine qua non* of our contract with the audience. We can't stand still in our development of new platforms, but it is vital that we modernise around these traditional values. And this is not to be nostalgic. Along with distinctive output, it is the factor that will distinguish and define us.

Is that it, then? Sorted? Unlikely. Producers are human and humans are fallible. What matters is not that there are occasional mistakes or lapses of judgement – because there will be – but that they are dealt with quickly and openly. Because trust in this context is not just about output, it is also about behaviour. Externally, that means the highest levels of accountability and transparency – so that when things do go wrong the public trusts the BBC to handle it effectively, openly and with humility. Internally, it means maintaining a culture and value system that puts trust and integrity at its heart.

Nietzsche said: 'What upsets me is not that you lied to me, but that from now on I can longer believe you.' So, one year on, what are the long term effects on the BBC's contract with its audience? Thankfully, public surveys since last summer would seem to suggest that trust in the BBC is resilient, as is faith in the BBC's ability and determination to tackle the issues effectively.

The events of last summer were traumatic, but in the long-term they have done us a favour. For the BBC it has been hard but, ultimately, therapeutic. The reason is summed up by a young participant in the final focus group: 'The BBC has the reputation for being the best broadcaster in the world. If they lose that then they're screwed.'

- **Vin Ray is the first director of the recently formed BBC College of Journalism. Joining the BBC in 1987, he worked as a producer on the *Nine O'Clock News* before becoming a foreign field producer, working abroad on many stories, including the first Gulf War, the Gorbachev coup, and the Bosnian war. He became foreign editor in 1993 and in 1996 he was asked to merge the newsgathering operations of the World Service and the domestic News and Current Affairs, becoming the first person to take charge of the BBC's entire foreign newsgathering operations. For several years, he had the additional role of recruiting and coaching all on-air talent for BBC News. He is the author two books: *The Reporter's Friend*; and the *TV News Handbook*.**

Chapter 14

How changes to HE media programmes can help restore trust

Media literacy means much more than the technical skills needed to edit film or to wow your friends on YouTube. It also means understanding how central the media are to the workings of a modern democracy and how dangerous it is when the media cannot be trusted, according to Roger Laughton, deputy chair of the British Film Institute

Entry into the broadcasting industry remains, as it always has been, anarchic. As a consequence, newcomers have not necessarily been exposed to any structured preparation for the range of problems and dilemmas they will face in the task of reflecting and recording the world in which we live. Yet media training and education programmes at modern universities have mushroomed. This short essay considers the arguments for and against a move towards greater 'professionalism' – a move in which media programmes in higher education could play a key role.

Some of us are old enough to remember the 'More Means Worse' debate. Faced with a limited expansion of British university student numbers at a time when less than 10 per cent of the eligible age group had access to higher education, Kingsley Amis and others argued that such expansion would inevitably lead to falling standards.

Looking back, it now seems obvious that more means neither better nor worse. It means more. It also means we now have a variety of league tables and comparators to enable aspiring students, parents and teachers to reach judgements about the quality of the education provided across the HE sector as a whole. Above all, it means many industries, including the media, recruit almost exclusively from university campuses.

Many HE programmes now include the words 'media', 'broadcasting' or 'journalism' in their titles. Implicit is the hint they will provide a springboard to a career in broadcasting or journalism. But, in the main, this is not so. As yet the media industries have developed few, if any, formal employment links with higher education, except in specialist areas like computer animation where graduates can learn specific skills. Indeed, some leading media professionals take a dim view of media courses, arguing that traditional degrees such as English

Literature and History are more likely to serve their need for talented and imaginative recruits.

Would a consensus over HE knowledge and skills be a chimera at best?
Media and communications programmes in HE vary widely from the strongly vocational to the purely academic. There is no consensus about what knowledge and skills a student can expect to have acquired at the conclusion of a degree programme.

Does this matter? Given that standardisation is impossible to achieve and possibly undesirable, it is easy to argue that any consensus would be a chimera at best. Yet employer-led organisations have been seeking in recent years to identify and badge those programmes and faculties which meet their own definition of standards. Student journalists have three accreditation schemes with which to comply. The Skillset Screen and Media Academies are a more recent attempt to identify excellence.

This overall approach, aiming to ensure industries have access to the skills essential to competitiveness, is part of a historical process in which industries, as they mature, recognise the need to train the next generation. Vocational programmes emerge, seeking to create and define the standards to which entrants should aspire. Lawyers, doctors, architects – all have developed professional bodies to monitor a range of qualifications which ensure they attract trained graduates with specific skills. At the same time maturity has been accompanied by an instinct to limit entry in order to ensure hard-earned skills are not valued too cheaply. Professionals have a habit of pulling up ladders behind them to prevent supply exceeding demand. Common sense suggests the media would not be an exception, if it took that route.

Perhaps the Fourth Estate is different? It thrives on freedom of expression. Should it be shackled by the conventions and protectionist tendencies of the traditional professions? When lawyers get it wrong, people go to prison. When nurses and doctors get it wrong, people die. Does anyone really suffer if broadcasters and journalists get it wrong in the free information markets of a democratic society?

I would argue we all suffer. A fraud in which five million phone-in voters are cheated of the cost of a £1 phone call is just as pernicious as a fraud in which one person steals five million pounds. Free societies are at high risk when you are cheated by the information messengers. Sloppy editorial standards also undermine the work of correspondents and crews, dozens of whom pay the ultimate sacrifice in order to tell us the truth about what's happening in the world's danger spots.

The crack embedded in the fabric of British broadcasting
The crisis of trust in the summer of 2007 was a symptom of a crack embedded in the fabric of British broadcasting. Current affairs broadcasters like to see themselves as descendants of Ed Murrow and Richard Dimbleby. But their colleagues in the entertainment departments have emerged from the cacophony of the music hall and the fairground where all is not what it seems and the show must go on.

Once upon a time, the two traditions co-existed, not always comfortably, within a single institution. Any suggestion that news programmes should mimic the formulas and rhythms of variety programmes would have been treated with disdain in the Broadcasting House of the fifties. But competition for primetime audiences ensured that divisions between the news and entertainment genres became blurred as soon as the BBC found itself faced with competition from ITV. Compare and contrast the *Panorama* of 1954 with the *Panorama* of 1964. Departments within the BBC may not have recognised it at the time, but popular television demanded a tabloid approach. Tim Hewat's *World in Action* and Derrick Amoore's *Nationwide* bred a generation of programme-makers for whom the lines dividing news and entertainment were close together.

Regulation by the BBC's governors and the Independent Broadcasting Authority ensured – for the most part – that the dividing lines remained in place, even if they were sometimes re-defined. Factual entertainment in the seventies and eighties came from the Current Affairs and Documentary departments of the public service broadcasters. There were checks and balances as well as an unspoken instinct that commercial market pressures should not impact on broadcast content. The broadcast media were trusted as they operated underneath a vast regulatory umbrella.

The 1990 Broadcasting Act sounded the death knell for that duopoly, by then already challenged by cable and satellite competition. Programme-makers, trained under the old system, may have had an instinct for what was right. But, as channels multiplied, so did the chances of production teams taking short cuts in search of ratings. Regulators stopped being nannies and turned into traffic policemen. 'Queengate' was an accident waiting to happen. It was headline news because it demonstrated that the world's most trusted broadcaster, the BBC, was capable of getting something badly wrong in an area where any mistake makes instant headlines. It was accompanied by numerous examples of malpractice in phone-in programmes across all the public service broadcasters, where viewers and listeners competed for prizes they had no chance of winning and voted in contests which had already closed.

Looking harder at how we select, educate and train recruits to the media industries

The events of 2007 explain why there is a strong case for looking harder at how we select, educate and train recruits for the creative and media industries. As they mature, the media industries are beginning to recognise that trust is the key to long-term commercial and creative success. Now they must also recognise that they need to take a lead, either directly or by working within professional associations, to ensure future entrants understand the responsibilities they will carry for telling the truth, not just in words but in their choice of sounds and images.

What's needed is an acceptance that media literacy means much more than the technical skills needed to edit film or to wow your friends on YouTube. It also means understanding how central the media are to the workings of a modern democracy and how dangerous it is when the media cannot be trusted.

In practice, what can be done? The BBC, now more than ever the dominant beast in the broadcasting jungle, continues to play a central role. Its training activities are central to its public purposes. It remains committed to the highest standards, as its vigorous response to the phone-in scandals of 2007 demonstrated. Elsewhere, there is now a Broadcast Training and Skills Regulator (BTSR), established by Ofcom to address the needs of the wider industry. So far its interventions have been limited, as it defines its role. But it has a remit to take an overview of the industry.

I should like to see the BBC and the BTSR get together with other interested parties Skillset, the National Union of Journalists, the Royal Television Society – to identify the key skills we should expect all media professionals to possess. These might include :

- an understanding of the impact and responsibilities of the mass media;
- specific skills in at least one specialist area;
- knowledge of the laws governing the operation of the mass media;
- demonstrable ability to work as an effective member of a team.

The need for properly trained tutors in HE

HE media programmes would be encouraged to ensure their graduates acquire these skills from properly trained tutors. Recruits from other academic disciplines would be expected to reach an equivalent skills level when they enter the industry. Skillset would have a specific responsibility for freelance training. In this scenario, HE and mainstream media would work much more closely with each other than now. The intention would not be to subvert the academic purposes of HE programmes but to ensure that the skills training, included in most media programmes, meets the needs of the industry. Professional bodies, like the Royal Television Society, might broker these relationships.

The objectives should be clear-cut – to ensure future media professionals understand how best they can play their part in the development of a highly-skilled responsible workforce and to provide a steady stream of industry recruits with generic and specific skills suitable for a career in media.

Who knows? Maybe one day broadcasters will have a Hippocratic Oath of their own. But not, I suspect, for some time yet.

- **Roger Laughton is deputy chair of the British Film Institute, chair of South West Screen and a member of the governing boards of the Arts Institute of Bournemouth and Metfilm. Between 1999 and 2005, he was Head of Bournemouth Media School. Previously he worked for the BBC for 25 years as producer, director and executive – and for ITV for nine years as CEO of Meridian and, from 1996, CEO of United Broadcasting and Entertainment.**

Chapter 15

Why it's so important to teach 'commitment to trustworthy reporting'

Kevin Marsh, editor of the BBC College of Journalism, argues that teaching journalists how to be trusted means teaching not rules but a mindset – one shared with the public they need to trust them

A documentary team is making a prestigious, big-name natural history series and they want to show the life cycle of a particular sea creature. Trouble is, no-one's ever filmed the female of the species laying her eggs, not in the wild at least: the eggs are laid too deep, too far from shore and too unpredictably. It would cost a fortune even to try to film and the chance of failure is high.

But they *can* film the egg-laying in an aquarium. And with some careful work in the cutting room and a bit of digital nudging they can produce a sequence that looks as if it were all filmed in the wild – knowing that every marine biologist would attest that the life cycle they show accords with every known scientific observation. The programme doesn't mention that the eggs were filmed being laid in an aquarium. Do you trust them?

OK, try this. A reporter has shot some footage of an unusual sport – ice yachting: it'll make a great end-of-bulletin-piece. Trouble is, when the reporter and editor look at the pictures in the edit the yachts don't seem to be going at anything like the speed they seemed to go in reality. So they crank up the speed of the tape until the yachts appear to be skidding around the frozen lake as fast as they did to the naked eye. On-air, the reporter doesn't mention the manipulation. Do you trust them?

Now, neither of these cases are hardest media dilemmas. But they're both real-life case studies that two different organisations have used to teach broadcasters how to be trusted: the first by the BBC College of Journalism in its *Safeguarding Trust* ethical teaching programme; the second by the American Radio and Television News Directors' Association.

Both get right to the heart of the 'trust' problem: journalists and media producers take the shapeless, endless raw material that is the world and cut, shape and form it into 'stories' – articles, films, bulletins or newspapers. And they do it in dark places where the public can't see what they're doing, have no way of knowing whether they can trust them or not.

When the most important question is left unanswered

In fact, it's difficult to say in the abstract what makes media trusted. And when pollsters ask the public whether they trust the people who make it – in polls in which journalists as a class, though not broadcasters, routinely finish close to bottom – the most important half of the question is left unasked: 'Trust to do what?'

'To tell the truth' or 'to be fair' are easy but misleading answers. And though they do go in the right direction, telling the 'truth' about MMR (that it doesn't cause autism) at the height of that particular (media-led) panic would not have brought automatic public trust in the teller: nor would 'being fair' to Gary Glitter rather than hunting and hounding him. And anyway, the idea of teaching what is truth brings its own problems.

Giambattista Vico isn't, but should be, the patron saint of journalism. His 17th century dictum 'verum ipsum factum est' should be engraved on the back of every journalist's mobile phone – of the few left who read Latin, anyway. 'Truth itself is a made thing' would have to do for the rest.

So the question for anyone devising a way to teach journalists how to do their job in a way the public can trust isn't how to tell an objective 'truth'; it's how they make the 'made thing' in a way that can be trusted, knowing that to the public it will look and feel like a kind of truth? If it were just about devising rules or principles, it would be simplicity itself.

By different routes and for different reasons, American journalism (unregulated) and British terrestrial broadcasters (regulated) have generated comprehensive guidelines and codes of journalistic behaviour that set out trusted behaviours with varying degrees of thoroughness and severity – effectively, undertakings to their audiences by which their trustworthiness can be judged.

These codes – like the BBC's *Editorial Guidelines* – capture well something approaching the principles of media behaviour that would generate trust: it's no accident that British terrestrial broadcasters (regulated, with published codes) are much more trusted than British newspapers (unregulated, most with no published code apart from the risible Press Complaints Commission's 'Editors' Code', which has much on common with the Flytipper's Guide to Environmental Protection).

Opening the '...gates' of ethical controversy

But it isn't just about rules or codes or learning how to apply their principles. The many '...gates' that necessitated the BBC's ethical teaching programme *Safeguarding Trust* (Queengate, BluePetergate I & II, Phonegate etc) happened in spite of the *Editorial Guidelines* that made it clear that the behaviours in question were unlikely to be found trustworthy by the public.

The problem is mindset. And something curious has happened to the media's: we see it every day. Its practitioners – chronically and ubiquitously in the press, acutely and occasionally in broadcasting – have managed to persuade themselves that their ethical universe is somehow different from the one that everyone else inhabits.

In her 2002 Reith Lectures, Professor Onora O'Neill (2003) listed why the British media are so distrusted for:

> editing and reporting that smears, sneers and jeers, names, shames and blames ... some misrepresents, some denigrates, some teeters on the brink of defamation. In this curious world, commitments to trustworthy reporting are erratic.

A curious world, indeed. When MORI surveyed British editors[i] only one in six of those questioned thought 'maintaining quality/integrity/standards' was the most important part of their job. If not theirs, whose? Two thirds thought 'increased competition for shrinking attention' was more important – and if Nick Davies (2008) is even partly right in *Flat Earth News*, it's a mindset that is, if anything, even more prevalent amongst editors in 2008.

And this slide into Millwallism ('nobody loves us, we don't care') isn't mere delinquency. Journalism's journey – in Professor Larry Sabato's (1991) description – from 'lapdog, through watchdog to junkyard dog' with all that entails in loss of public trust is, in part at least, legitimised by a strand of academic thinking. Professor Adrian Monck of City University, London, concluded in his book *Can you trust the media* (2008) that we were misguided even to think that we should.

His somewhat nihilistic view can be boiled down to this (and I concede I'm caricaturing rather than characterising – but it's not a million miles off, trust me): trust is a deception; we don't need to trust journalists – in fact, we don't need them at all but if they insist on hanging around, let's see them as no more than the attention seeking storytellers they are. Trust doesn't come into it.

We journalism educators who think trust *does* matter – how can we trust anything about the world if we can't trust the media through which we learn about it? – inevitably ask ourselves, then, how long can any lesson in trust stick when the prevailing mindset in newsroom after newsroom doesn't just fall short of the ideal, it denies such an ideal even exists?

On the importance of 'fitting in'
Mike Jempson is director of the MediaWise Trust – an independent media watchdog, now in its fifteenth year, originally set up by people who saw themselves victims of the media. He also teaches journalists in, among other things, the ethics of a trade he would like to see more trusted. But ...:

> ...the success of a college depends on how many people it gets into work at the other end, so the pressure is on to produce people who will fit – fit the sort of jobs that are available.[ii]

'Fitting in' apparently includes adopting that alternative ethical universe. Mike Jempson adds:

> Somebody once said to me, 'You know who's going to employ someone who's won a prize on journalism ethics?' Very few people, in fact. Ethics, people say, is what happens on a Friday, late on a Friday afternoon, on journalism courses.[iii]"

Hardly surprising, then, that mendacity figures so large in newspaper journalism's recent story: newspapers which can't get to truth's first base over a royal prostate (*Evening Standard*), or over the McCanns (Richard Desmond's four *Express* and *Star* titles – not once but more than a hundred times); or the royal reporter who couldn't understand that bugging phones is illegal as well as a breach of trust (Clive Goodman at the *News of the World* ... and, according to the information commissioner Richard Thomas, three-hundred journalists on other papers).

These egregious examples of untrustworthiness – along with Professor O'Neill's more workaday account – are a direct result of that mindset: the belief that somehow the media inhabit an ethical universe that is separate from – at best parallel to, at worst in conflict with – the one everyone else inhabits.

It begins with well-intentioned broadcasters telling themselves it's OK to cut in those aquarium shots because the artifice – ahem, deception – enables them to demonstrate a bigger truth; and if the audience knows that without a bit of trickery they'd have nothing at all ... well, they'll probably buy it. And indeed, many do: but that doesn't mean those audiences don't see it as a bargain with the broadcaster in which the deal is: if/when we know how you did this, we'd still trust you.

But if it's OK to fake a film sequence to demonstrate a bigger scientific 'truth' … how big a stretch is it, ethically, to reconstructing a news event to show 'how it almost certainly happened', based on sources you believe to be 'true'? And how big a stretch from that to running a newspaper story about the health of an elderly royal that seems more likely than not to be 'true'?

Why teaching principles is only the beginning

So can we teach trust? On balance, yes: but we have to recognise that teaching a set of rules or principles is only the beginning – the easy bit. As with *Safeguarding Trust,* rules, codes and guidelines are a good starting place – so long as they're fixed in the ethical universe that audiences inhabit rather than the one some journalists and media professionals have constructed for themselves.

And more than anything, we and our charges need to understand that the truly important thing to teach is what Professor O'Neill calls 'commitment to trustworthy reporting'. Teaching that produces a few bright points of contrast in what the public see as a self-regarding, self-justifying, ethically bleak media mindset isn't enough. We have to change that mindset; convince the sceptics within the media that trust does matter and persuade leaders in the industry that their role is to maintain integrity and standards as well as market share.

Only then will the media in general and journalists in particular start to climb up instead of sinking even further down that trust table.

Notes

[i] MORI Key Audience Research: Survey of British Editors, 2004
[ii] Interview with author for *Analysis* on BBC Radio 4, 3 July 2008
[iii] Ibid

References

Davies, N, (2008) *Flat Earth News*, London, Chatto and Windus

Monck, A. (2008) *Can you trust the media?*, London, Icon Books

O'Neill, O. (2002) BBC Reith Lectures 2002 *A question of trust.* Available online at *http://www.bbc.co.uk/radio4/reith2002/lecture5.shtml*

Sabato, L. (1991) *Feeding Frenzy: How Attack Journalism has Transformed American Politics,* New York, Free Press

- Kevin Marsh is editor of the BBC College of Journalism and a former editor of *Today*, *The World at One*, *The World This Weekend*, *PM* and *Broadcasting House*. In July 2008, he wrote and presented an edition of *Analysis* on BBC Radio 4 entitled 'Responsible Journalism'.

Section 5. Afterword

Picnics on Vesuvius: the media and the problem of trust

It is time to liberate that old dog, Diogenes of Sinope, from the condescension and contempt of posterity. We need Diogenes, the cynic, the corrosive doubter of everything. Not in full measure, but with a comfortable muzzle. For moderate cynicism is a vital part of a vibrant democratic culture, argues John Tulloch in this wide-ranging and critical overview of the 'media trust' debate

Raised in this uneasy and politicised culture, the engravers and printshop proprietors must surely have been critically opinionated...Whatever their spirit, whether genial or savage, their ceaseless wry commentaries on abuses of power and on double standards, their incessant lampooning of princes and statesmen, their repetitive equation of Foxites with Jacobins, their lip-smacking exposure of high-born vices – all these could not but subvert the dignity of established hierarchies and even the sacrality of royalty. In their constant barrage, it's not difficult to discern that notion of the public good that many continentals thought of as essentially English: sceptical of high pretensions and habitually disrespectful – the inherited cast of mind many of us, to the bemusement of others, still live by, largely for the better, though politicians and celebrities disagree.
  Vic Gatrell (2006: 141)

Who was the most trusted commentator on the 2008 US presidential elections? According to the *Observer* it was Jon Stewart, who nightly in *The Daily Show* delivered stories 'with lacerating humour and an inbuilt bullshit detector' (Smith 2008: 32). Claimed journalist David Smith: 'They [US viewers] know Stewart will part politicians from their reputations with laser-like precision, while simultaneously rubbing the media's nose in its own deference. And most importantly, they trust him.'

The first source Smith wheeled into place was a 36-year-old astronomy teacher: '*The Daily Show* is probably more reliable for news than anything on TV except PBS,' said Barry McKernan. 'It stands apart from everything else because it unspins the news. It frankly points out how ridiculous the 24-hour news networks are – mostly gassing away by unqualified "experts" filling the hours' (Smith op.cit).

A week is a long time in the unpicking of the culture of irrational exuberance. Take a seismic financial crisis and the debate about the much-lamented decline of trust begins to wear a bogus aspect. That great English tradition of 'the common man's contempt for the great' (Gatrell 2006: 519) reasserts itself. The argument that "'Trust" was always a figleaf for power' (Beckett this volume) gains allure. As markets melt and banks buckle we rediscover (if we ever lost them) the simple virtues of cynicism – quibbles about the issue of trust in the media become insignificant in relation to the Crisis of Trust in the economic system. Of course, there must be a point where shares in trust are so outrageously cheap that they might be worth…a flutter.

As a concept, Trust is a slippery customer, rich in promises and poor in delivery. It is easy enough to see that what she wants is a relationship, between a *trustor* and a *trustee*. And it is plausible that Trust's respectable but fervent cousin is Faith, who has generally needed the sisterly support of Hope (aka Confidence) and Charity (in *New English Bible* parlance, Love). If we are lucky, we feel we know Trust intimately: many people derive an understanding of her from the sphere of their private life. But the trust we may be fortunate enough to be able to give and share with parent, partner or friend is generally the only instance of its operation as an absolute. Being *trusting* outside the private sphere is a synonym for foolishness.

Trust's main guises: Dozy and Grumpy
Or we might argue that Trust presents herself in two main guises – Dozy and Grumpy. Dozy rests beside the domestic hearth, and is a sleeping partner in our routine social interactions. Grumpy is wideawake, out on the streets, and on the lookout for dangers. We might anatomise her further. Dozy perhaps has two aspects: Lazy and Passionate. Lazy just assumes things are OK, and can't be fagged to check. She doesn't want to interrogate her habits. And of course Passionate, not lazy at all, doesn't want to entertain doubts.

Streetwise Grumpy is both Vigilant and Anxious. Anxious fears something is wrong, is risk-averse, looks for evidence to confirm her fears, and may abruptly hightail it. Vigilant is more robust, alert to non-performance, keen on codes, and proceeds consistently on the basis of reasonable expectation.

In everyday life we have few alternatives to Dozy and become Grumpy only by experience. As we know, grumpiness increases with age. Until our savings are imperilled by a bank that suddenly becomes dodgy, we have to keep our money somewhere. Northern Rock (the first British banking failure since Overend and Gurney in the 1860s) stripped some British people of their comfort blanket of banking probity. Ordinary people contemplated cash under the mattress, or escapes into gold (a taxi driver advised me that this latter was The Best Thing). As they queued round the block to get their savings out, many Britons became distinctly grumpy.

Likewise we have to live somewhere. We put Grumpy to sleep as we enter our bricks and mortar. Until our safe houses shake, and we discover we live in a (thankfully mild) earthquake zone, as peaceful Lincolnshire did one night in 2008. Or the dodgy bank (perhaps now owned in Spain) forecloses the mortgage.

Is Trust rational? Sir Thomas Browne observed in the 1640s that 'so large is the Empire of Truth, that it hath place within the walls of Hell, and the Devils themselves are daily forced to practise it… they lie not unto each other; as well understanding that all community is continued by Truth, and that of Hell cannot consist without it.' (Browne [1646] Book 1, Ch 11). Browne's contemporary Hobbes's reading of human nature and its competitive 'restlesse desire of Power after power that ceaseth onely in Death' (Hobbes 1985 [1651] 161) was such that he argued our mutual fear forced us to accept the artificial structure of the state, 'a Common Power…one man, or…one Assembly of men, that may reduce all their Wills…unto one Will' (Hobbes op cit. 227). The constructed Trust in Leviathan or 'the mortall God' of the state allowed society to be possible.

The rational exercise of individual autonomy

This notion that trust produces a collective benefit is central to the Enlightenment philosophers, whose intellectual inheritors include neo-Kantians like Baroness Onora O'Neill. She utilises the concept of informed consent as a 'hallmark' which 'presupposes and expresses' trust between strangers and enables the rational exercise of individual autonomy and independence in the market place (O'Neill 2002 and see O'Hara 2004: 42-9). For O'Neill the scope of informed consent is very wide, from the trust which is given when accompanied with a rational understanding of the complexities of a pension plan or mortgage, to our everyday dealings:

> We give informed consent in face-to-face transactions too, though we barely notice it. We buy apples in the market, we exchange addresses with acquaintances, we sit down for a haircut. It sounds very pompous to speak of these daily transactions as based on informed consent, yet in each we assume that the other party is neither deceiving nor coercing (O'Neill op cit).

This is the trustor as Vigilant, an alert rational consumer, dependent on the integrity of the messages sent her by the information market. But like many Enlightenment discussions, this rationality retains the luxury of the intellectual salon or the academic senior common room. Buying apples in the market forsooth: the Platonic guardian leaving her baronic perch to jostle in the market with the rest of us. As E.M. Forster finely observed in Chapter 5 of *Howard's*

End: 'To trust people is a luxury in which only the wealthy can indulge; the poor cannot afford it' (Forster 2000 [1910]). Add to that 'poor' the pensioners with shares in Bradford and Bingley or Northern Rock.

Are the roots of Trust rational at all? 'What is remarkable about trust is how *little* rationality (in the self-interested sense) seems to be involved in our decisions to trust.' (O'Hara 2004: 260). Doziness as a fact of life. Among the most seductive metaphors are those that liken childhood growth to developments in the social sphere. Thus the celebrated social scientist Anthony Giddens, discussing the salience of trust – in face-to-face relationships with family members and immediate others – in the formation of the child's identity, slides easily to a comparison with the role of trust is the operation of those abstract systems – politics, media etc – that he argues help to form a *civic* identity (Giddens 1990). If you don't trust your politicians you can't be an authentic citizen. They not only want your vote, they want your Trust. Unsurprisingly we discover there's not much of it about. What there is, is fragile. Enter a stage army of academics and pollsters. The conventional wisdom of the times became that trust in social institutions, parliament, and press is on the decline and that this is A Bad Thing. (O'Neill op cit, Lloyd 2004).

Journalists – bottom of the league for truth-telling

The MORI veracity Index (Worcester 2004), running since 1983, has consistently put British journalists at the bottom of league for truth-telling. In 1983 just 19 per cent of respondents expected them to generally tell the truth, compared to 73 per cent who didn't. In 2003 the figures were about the same (18 per cent against 75 per cent) but it had fluctuated during the twenty years to as low as 10 per cent who trusted journalists and 79 per cent who thought they were generally, well, liars (both in 1993). At the same time the number of people who say they trust doctors and teachers has actually increased – 91 per cent generally trusted doctors in 2003 and 87 per cent teachers.

These figures are well known but there is nothing else so empirical that we can deploy as evidence to chart the longer term alleged decline of trust in the media. And they are subject to the usual provisos about sample surveys. We do know something of the career of the concept 'journalist' in English and indeed of 'Grub Street'. On the whole that does not support the concept of decline, at least in Britain. Journalists may plume themselves on their professionalism but the grimy epithets clinging to the term do not suggest a straightforward descent from trustworthiness to deceitfulness. In England the expression 'Gentlemen of the press' has generally been a sly joke at journalism's expense.

It is a fair bet that the English public sphere of Habermasian fancy – based on an ahistorical reading of the function of 18th century coffee houses, newspapers, and public debate – never furnished much trust in the veracity or transparency of discourse but involved verification techniques similar to a village (consider the size of London in the 18th century and the relative size of the literate class). John Brewer observes of the London press of the mid to late 18th century – contemporary with Boswell – that 'the newspaper was not an authoritative organ, written by professionals to offer objective information to the public, but a place where public rumour, news and intelligence could circulate as if it were printed conversation. Many commentators believed that the enormous growth in news, fuelled by the business interests of the newspaper proprietors and lacking any check on its veracity, created a climate of scandal and sensation' (Brewer 2004: 40-1). Boswell himself used his journalistic activities to settle scores, promote himself, and generally make mischief.

The GrubSteety, tacky, hacky reality of journalism

The juggernautian public sphere concept may well be (perish the thought) closer to the ivory tower (or by now cyber silo) of the peer reviewed academic journal than the GrubStreety, tacky, hacky, self-promoting commercial reality of journalism. Coffee houses and pubs were not sites primarily of rational debate but entertainment, laughter, mockery. If they were a great focus for the production of civility they were also breeding grounds for rumour, crime and mayhem.

The decline of trust in the press has of course been a theme of public discourse for at least the best part of a century. In the case of the British media the decline of trust can be variously located to at least four distinct periods. For some the rot started with the creation of the powerful and unscrupulous model of Edwardian New Journalism and tabloid sensationalism epitomised by Northcliffe's ceaseless campaigning and desire to 'work up' issues, from invasions to health scares (Clarke 1931: 54).

For others the '60s is a plausible candidate, with the growth of partisan dealignment, the end of social deference and the mutation – in the UK at least – of traditional class-based allegiances and structures of feeling. Pirate radio, alternative newspapers and 'New Journalism' all registered a decline in trust for the conventional media.

Or there is the 1980s and the successful promotion of a freemarket gospel of privatisation and globalisation, creating world-encompassing media empires and eliminating armies of journalists in favour of a celebrity-driven promotional culture. A recent and most eloquent example of this latter argument is Nick Davies's book *Flat Earth News* (Davies 2008).

His key finding – backed up by research conducted by the school of journalism at Cardiff University – is that while British newspaper pagination has undoubtedly mushroomed, the number of journalists has shrunk dramatically. Journalists have therefore substantially less time to conduct their own research, check stories and verify facts. Davies constructs a powerful account of the destruction of the role of the journalists who actually *got out of the office*: an Old Contemptible Army of local reporters, freelances and news agencies who had created a dense newsgathering network across the UK. He chronicles a twenty-year erosion of this network of local journalists and news agencies, together with the undermining of BBC local and regional journalism by ferocious staff cuts, and the advent of a promotional culture where handouts, PR briefings, and the heavy use of a small number of news agencies (principally the Press Association and Reuters) determines the bulk of coverage.

Among other things, the Cardiff researchers surveyed 2000 news stories published in Fleet Street's five leading dailies. They found that 70 per cent of home news stories were either wholly or partially rewritten from Press Association or other wire copy. This was also found in 65 per cent of broadcast news stories.

The influence of PA on the formation of Flat Earth News

The Cardiff researchers found 'that 30 per cent of the home news stories in the five most prestigious Fleet Street titles were direct rewrites of copy from PA or smaller wire agencies' and that 70 per cent of homes news stories contained at least some wire copy (ibid: 74). Davies reveals: 'So great is the influence of PA that I know reporters who have had a story rejected by their news desks and have discreetly called PA, given them the story and waited it to run on the wire, at which point their news desks have asked them to follow it up' (ibid: 75). On the influence of public relations on news the Cardiff researchers claim that PR material found its way into 54 per cent of news stories (ibid: 91). In many cases the stories were barely rewritten from handouts. Only 20 per cent of stories appeared to involve any original research by the journalist.

This argument is for the emergence of a promotional media culture, with journalists dutifully subbing PR handouts and the construction of news largely migrating to the corporations and official bodies that provide the advertising. It is, of course, in neither side's interest to explore this relationship, although a plausible reason therefore for the decline in circulation may not be the migration of readers to internet sites but the fact that they are not unaware of the lack of news or the heavy promotional spin of the news that remains. Davies's book was predictably rubbished by journalist reviewers such as the former *Times* editor columnist Sir Simon Jenkins, who claimed Davies was arguing for a 'golden age' of reporting that never existed (Jenkins 2008). Other commentators such as Sir

Harold Evans, the former editor of *The Sunday Times*, seem to accept the thesis (see for example interview on BBC Radio 4, *Broadcasting House*, 16 March 2008). For other commentators the prime candidate for the start of the rot is not the '60s nor the '80s but the First World War. This is a well-established juncture to locate the decline of trust. Writing in the late 1920s, the poet Robert Graves recalled returning wounded to Blighty from the Western Front in 1916: 'We could not understand the war-madness that ran wild everywhere, looking for a pseudo-military outlet. The civilians talked a foreign language; and it was newspaper language. I found serious conversation with my parents all but impossible' (Graves 1999).

Historians such as Michael Redley argue that, after the war, as the public increasingly became aware of the nature of wartime propaganda, a 'crisis of trust' developed. C.E. Montague, a *Guardian* journalist who survived the trenches, described the prevalent postwar attitude as 'vigilant scepticism'. Certainly this was true for the intelligentsia, but then one cannot imagine the likes of Graves or Siegfried Sassoon swallowing whole the pre-war *Daily Mail* anyway, assuming it was even on their radar.

How trust is shaped by our apprehension of various genres

There are other larger issues about the media and trust: we can distinguish between the vast range of routine factual information carried by the modern media, which we generally trust in an unreflecting Dozy way (football scores, stock prices, even weather reports), and the category of 'news', about which we may be more Vigilant. (Of course, newspapers notoriously get numbers wrong.) Trust in a newspaper is not a simple thing, but multifoliate and shaped by our apprehension of the various genres, categories of information and differing modes of address that make up the entire complex artefact. The 'trust' I deploy in regard to a bullying front page lead in the *Sun* will be different in kind to my scrutiny of the weather map or football results, my amused contemptuous fascination with Jeremy Clarkson's column and my immersion in Dear Deidre's problem page.

The same basic point applies to a newspaper that positively plumes itself on its integrity such as the *Guardian*. Who else would/could give away (on 29 September 2008) a mug bearing the inscription: 'Owned by no one. Free to say anything.' If only. We may, perhaps, suspect its newswriting, loath its high opinion of itself, prefer the sport in the *Sun* but treasure Hadley Freeman or Simon Jenkins, and deploy a playful possessiveness which can mingle with contempt. That is, we can read a newspaper and also despise it.

This playful suspicion or contempt of course is not enough for O'Neill, who argues that 'newspaper journalists face few disciplines that support public trust' and 'there are no enforceable requirements for accuracy or coverage and balance; there are no enforceable requirements to refrain from writing on subjects of which they are ignorant; there are no enforceable requirements to distinguish reporting from commentary… There is a well-guarded "right" to hide sources, that can be used to obstruct the reader's ability to tell whether there is any sources whatsoever, or (if there is) whether it can be trusted' (O'Neill 2002a: 175 -6).

Many newspaper readers no doubt have entertained similar notions – just force the wretched Bennetts and Aaronovitchs not to write about stuff of which they are ignorant. Make the lot of them get a proper journalistic job. But only a philosopher would seriously argue it. Just whose Platonic Guardian would check the ignorance of the hack? How precisely would 'reporting' be distinguished from 'commentary'?

And precisely what would Authority be up to while the hacks were being licensed, or subject to enforceable fact-checking? In a useful recent collection which hopefully titles our times, *An Age of Suspicion*, Bakir and Barlow argue that:

> Given that in the contemporary public sphere, there is minimal interest in forming a public…but every intention to inform and indoctrinate one for political and economic gains; given that government and business have professionalized their communications; and given that this strategic communication non-transparently subsidises and co-opts media, the public are right to withhold their trust from both the power holders and the media (Bakir and Barlow 2007: 210).

Is there a light at the end of the postmodern tunnel? Not much

In fact, they say that the public should probably distrust power holders more than they do. Is there any light at the end of this post-modern tunnel? Not much. Although new media offer some promise in promoting access and transparency, allowing the creation of online publics and avoiding the machinations of professional communicators, they are pessimistic about the prospects as it is colonised by corporate forces. The 'public should be *more* distrustful of new media – and if they are not yet, it will not be long before new media are tainted with the same aura of distrust as old media'.

What's left? They take refuge in the idea of independent regulatory bodies devising a system of 'transparency rankings' to audit media that are succumbing to PR and for digital photography to utilise image authentication technology which will reveal if the picture has been tampered with. Citizen juries on media, trust and accountability are also proffered and greater public involvement in the selection of members of regulatory quangos.

Such prescriptions are admirable but thin. After it climbs out of its present hole, or quietens down to a placid rumbling, global capitalism will infallibly penetrate any field where there is profit to be made. Regulatory bodies have served Britain well in defending the public interest in the narrow sector of terrestrial broadcasting but have failed dismally to regulate the press. They will be increasingly embattled and undermined in the convergent megachannel future. We may simply have to live without much trust in journalists and public bodies and to be alert to the possibility of systematic, deliberate deceit – public lying for power, profit or out of a self-righteous faith in one's own integrity. But that is nothing new.

Discussing the use of deceptive denials and cover stories by US politicians and administrators over the bombing of Cambodia and the Bay of Pigs invasion Sissela Bok quotes Irving Janis's explanation of the moral contortions of the wise and good in justifying systematic deceit:

> The members' firm belief in the inherent morality of their group and their use of undifferentiated negative stereotypes of opponents enable them to minimise decision conflicts between ethical values and expediency, especially when they are inclined to resort of violence. The shared belief that 'we are a wise and good group' inclines them to use group concurrence as a major criterion to judge the morality as well as the efficacy of any policy under discussion. 'Since our groups objectives are good,' the members feel 'any means we decide to use must be good' (Bok 1980: 97).

Are we more suspicious? Perhaps we simply have more information to enable us to be suspicious to some purpose. For those of us who feel we were bamboozled into a 'War on Terror' by systematic official deceit, this remains a sensitive time to be discussing trust. It is five years since the invasion of Iraq. News was recently released that former British Prime Minister Tony Blair (who has, *mirabile dictu*, set up a 'Faith Foundation'), is to teach about faith at Yale. His biographer states: 'His concern is faith as a part of public life...trying to bring people together as he did in Northern Ireland and as he tried in the Middle East' (Anthony Seldon, interview BBC Radio 4, 16 March 2008).

The quality of faith is defined by its purity and sincerity. The characteristic utterance of the faith-driven politician is 'I did it because it was right. I believed what I was doing.' Conveniently, this removes action from argument or question. Damn your sincerity (as we might indeed say to journalists). Where are your sources?

The distinction between scepticism and cynicism is illusory
It is time to liberate that old dog, Diogenes of Sinope, from the condescension and contempt of posterity. We need Diogenes, the cynic, the corrosive doubter of everything. Not in full measure, but with a comfortable muzzle. For moderate cynicism is a vital part of a vibrant democratic culture.

1. The distinction between scepticism and cynicism is illusory – they are near relatives. Scepticism is critical doubting of all propositions. Cynicism is critical doubting of all propositions with an assumption of bad faith or in modern parlance, false consciousness. Cynicism is a hard form of scepticism.

2. We are, hopefully, not sceptical of the people we love (or not much). That apart, scepticism should have no limits outside the private sphere of friends and family. Absolute cynicism embraces no limits, including the private sphere. It embraces both the lonely isolation of the world doubting hermit and the paranoid world of the megalomaniac dictator. Consider Strindberg's great and terrible play, *The Father*. This is not a world a person can survive in.

3. Systematic and critical doubting is a condition of a mature modern democracy. The antidote to spin is the assumption of systematic dishonesty and bad faith as a condition of positions of power. This entails moderate cynicism.

4. To prescribe social 'trust' is to support a class system based on a structured differential access to resources including resources of information and analysis. It is support a culture of insiders and outsiders. 'We' can be cynical, but 'they' (i.e. the mass of the population) need a fundamental level of 'trust' to keep the system rolling. Pretty soon, we'll have to find a way to get them investing again.

5. 'Trust' is not a condition of a vibrant public sphere. That fundamental condition is:
- a reasonable expectation of rule-governed behaviour – viz. sets of obligations and expectations (e.g. see Goffman 1972: 49) and
- a preparedness to enter into dialogue, in which laughter and mockery are established forms, as part of the 'play' of dialogue.

6. Dialogue does not assume or preclude mutual trust. The fundamental constitutive assumption is tolerance – a preparedness to hear the 'other side(s)'. Tolerance can subsist with moderate contempt.

7. In journalism this relates to an imperative to hear the 'other' side(s) of a story. This can be ritualistic in the assumption that there is a counterbalancing case that must be put and/or morally objectionable in the case of (say) blatant and systematic human rights abuse.

Cyclical capitalism is a device to put the resources of the many at the service of a few. It is historically subject to an alternation between the irrational exuberance of the South Sea Bubble and the irrational pessimism of the Great Depression: recurrent crises of confidence, prophecies of doom and the death of trust are the cost of picnicking on Vesuvius. As virtuous, moderate cynics, we should cultivate our friends.

References

Bakir, Vian and Barlow, David M. (eds) (2007) *Communication in the Age of Suspicion: Trust and the Media*, Basingstoke, Palgrave Macmillan

Bok, Sissela (1980 [1978]) *Lying. Moral Choice in Public and Private Life*, London, Quartet Books, paper edition

Brewer, John (2004) *Sentimental Murder. Love and Madness in the Eighteenth Century*, London, HarperCollins

Browne, Sir Thomas (1646) *Pseudodoxia Epidemica, or Vulgar Errors.* 6th edition of 1672. Available online at http://penelope.uchicago.edu/pseudodoxia/pseudo111.html

Clarke, Tom (1931) *My Northcliffe Diary*, London, Victor Gollancz

Davies, Nick (2008) *Flat Earth News*, London, Chatto and Windus

Forster, Edward Morgan (2000 [1910]) *Howard's End*, London, Penguin

Gatrell, Vic (2006) *City of Laughter. Sex and satire in Eighteenth-Century London*, London, Atlantic Books

Giddens, Anthony (1990) *The Consequences of Modernity*, Cambridge, Polity Press

Goffman, Erving (1972 [1967]) The Nature of Deference and Demeanour in *Interaction Ritual: Essays on Face-to-Face Behaviour*, Harmondsworth, Allen Lane (first published in USA, 1967)

Graves, Robert (1999 [1929]) *Goodbye to All That*, London, Penguin Books

Hobbes, Thomas (1968 [1651]) *Leviathan*, edited by Macpherson, C. B. London, Pelican Books

Jenkins, Simon (2008) No topic is so surrounded by myth as the golden age of the press, *Guardian*, 8 February. Available online at http://www.guardian.co.uk/commentisfree/2008/feb/08/politics.media, accessed 16 March 2008

Lloyd, John (2004) *What the Media are Doing to Our Politics*, London, Constable

Marx, Karl and Engels, Friedrich (2002 [1848]) *The Communist Manifesto*, London, Penguin Classics

O'Hara, Kieron (2004) *Trust from Socrates to Spin*, Cambridge, Icon Books

O'Neill, Onora (2002) *Licence to Deceive*, Lecture 5 of the Reith Lectures 2002. Available online at http://www.bbc.co.uk/print/radio4/reith2002/lecture5.shtml?print, accessed 11 October 2004

O' Neill, Onora (2002a) *Autonomy and Trust in Bioethics.* Cambridge, Cambridge University Press

Redley, Michael (2007) Origins of the Problem of Trust: Propaganda during the First World War, Bakir, Vian and Barlow, David M. (eds) *Communication in the Age of Suspicion: Trust and the Media*, Basingstoke, Palgrave Macmillan

Smith, David (2008) How a satirist became America's most influential TV personality, *Observer*, 14 September p.32

Worcester, Robert (2003) Whom Do We Trust? Neither Politicians Nor Journalists! Available online at http://www.mori.com/pubinfo/rmw/whomdowetrust.shtml, accessed 11 October 2004

- John Tulloch is professor of journalism and head of the School of Journalism, University of Lincoln. Previously he was chair of the Department of Journalism and Mass Communication at the University of Westminster. Recent work includes jointly editing, with Colin Sparks, *Tabloid Tales* (Maryland: Rowman and Littlefield 2000). He has written on press regulation, official news management, popular television and the press's coverage of the 'war on terror'. He has also had a chapter on the journalism of Charles Dickens in *The Journalistic Imagination: Literary Journalists from Defoe to Capote and Carter* (edited by Richard Keeble and Sharon Wheeler; Routledge 2007).

And finally

Ethical Space Book No. 2

Communication Ethics Now, drawing together articles from Volume 2 (2005) of *Ethical Space: The International Journal of Communication Ethics*, is published in November 2008. In a foreword, Cees Hamelink, professor emeritus of International Communication at the University of Amsterdam, comments: 'Ethical inquiry needs to be more creative and deconstruct situations that look like dilemmas into configurations of a wide variety of moral options and challenges. We are very fortunate to have such important platforms as *Communication Ethics Now* for this exercise in new forms of reflection!'

He adds: 'This book convincingly demonstrates how lively and relevant today's ethical reflections on communication can be. The chapters of the book cover such an exciting and broad range of topics.'

Edited by Richard Keeble, joint editor of *Ethical Space*, the 25 chapters are divided into five sections. In the first, which focuses on journalism ethics, John Tulloch examines the British press's coverage of the CIA torture flights (better known as 'extraordinary rendition') while Julie-ann Davies reports on the media's increasing use of anonymous sources. Jane Taylor takes a particularly unusual look at the media's obsession with celebrity focusing on the coverage of Carole Chaplin, Cherie Blair's 'style guru' and broadcaster, novelist and columnist Libby Purves expresses outrage at the media's daily diet of 'unkind intrusions and falsifications'.

In an international section, leading Nigerian academic Kate Azuka Omenugha explores the representation of Africanness in the British press, Susanne Fengler and Stephan Russ-Mohl express concern over the slump in media standards in Germany while Angelika W. Wyka focuses on journalistic standards and democratisation of the mass media in Poland, Hungary and the Czech Republic.

In a section that takes a historical perspective on journalism ethics, Jane Chapman's chapter looks at 'Republican Citizenship, Ethics and the French Revolutionary Press 1789-92' while Martin Conboy's focuses on Wooler's *Black Dwarf*, a radical journal of the early 19th century.

Another section on communication ethics and pedagogy draws on papers at the 2005 annual conference of the Institute of Communication Ethics with contributions from Raphael Cohen-Almagor, John Strain, Brian Hoey, Brian Morris, Simon Goldsworthy and Anne Gregory. The philosophical dimensions of communication ethics are explored by Karen Sanders, Hallvard Johannes Fossheim (in an interview with Kristine Lowe) Robert Beckett, Moira Carroll-Mayer and Bernd Carsten Stahl. In the final section on business and communication ethics, Kristine Lowe interviews Paul Jackson, of Manchester Business School.

Editor Richard Keeble, in an introduction, says: 'The Institute of Communication Ethics (ICE) stresses in its mission statement: "Communication ethics is the founding philosophy for human interaction that defines issues according to their impact on human well-being and relationships." And it is this caring for people – the desperately poor, the inarticulate, the oppressed – along with a sense that honesty, integrity, clarity, respect for difference and diversity are some of the core principles underlying human interaction and, ultimately, communication ethics that drive the many writings in this volume.'

- *Communication Ethics Now* **is published by Troubador, Leicester, for £12.99 For more details see:**
  http://www.troubador.co.uk/book_info.asp?bookid=623.
  It follows the success of *Communication Ethics Today,* **also published by Troubador, which drew on articles in the first volume of** *Ethical Space.* **See**
  http://www.troubador.co.uk/book_info.asp?bookid=296

Printed in the United Kingdom
by Lightning Source UK Ltd.
135895UK00002B/312/P